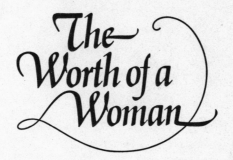

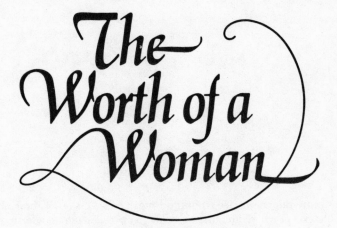

The Worth of a Woman

by
Iverna Tompkins

LOGOS INTERNATIONAL
Plainfield, New Jersey

Scripture quotations are from the King James Version of the Holy
Bible except where identified as: NAS (New American Standard) or
JB (The Jerusalem Bible).
A Scripture reference in a sentence does not necessarily mean the
words are an exact quotation, but that a similar thought of that of the
Scripture is being expressed.

Some material in chapters 2 and 3 was derived from the article,
"Woman," in *The International Standard Bible Encyclopaedia,* volume 5.
Copyright, 1939, 1956 by William B. Eerdmans Publishing Co.:
Grand Rapids, MI.

THE WORTH OF A WOMAN
Copyright © 1978 by Logos International
All Rights Reserved
Printed in the United States of America
Library of Congress Catalog Card Number: 78-70534
International Standard Book Number: 0-088270-256-4
Logos International, Plainfield, New Jersey 07060

To my daughter, Debbie, who is beautifully discovering the worth of womanhood.

Contents

Prayer

God of all men and women, Lord, who sent your Son to lift women from degradation and to forgive men who degraded them, break the stereotypes of our minds and cultures, so that we may see other people as you see them, and so we may be all that you have created us to be. Through Jesus Christ, in whom there is neither male nor female, we pray. . . . Amen.

(Dr. David Allan Hubbard, president of Fuller Theological Seminary, Pasadena, CA., and professor of Old Testament)

*Distinguishing the counterfeit from the real—
making up your own mind—avoiding extremes*

SECTION 1:

How Can I Know Who I Am?

Today's Christian woman has been hard pressed to find the balance between the biblical view of what it means to be a woman and the secular challenges confronting her. In these days of extremism, it is imperative to find this vital balance.

Those warring from the world's standpoint for women's rights have often taken an extreme position far beyond equal job opportunities or equal pay, leading to a stand of sameness or unisex. While we cannot accept this stand, we see that God has, through this new secular awareness of women, permitted a way to be paved for His women. People are beginning to listen as women speak to many issues and to accept their abilities in a far wider scope than before.

As God begins to bring fresh truth to the church, the enemy seeks to counterfeit it on a large scale. The believer must not be taken in by the counterfeit, but seek the real. The real in this case is *God's purposing for women to move into the fullness of His plan for them.*

Immaturity allows the believer to accept an extreme position or—like the proverbial ostrich with its head in the sand—deny that anything is being said.

Unfortunately, immaturity seems to be in the limelight today. It is seen in those who are verbally criticizing other believers and in choosing up of "sides" reminiscent of "I am of Paul; and I of Apollos; and I of Cephas; and I of Christ" (1 Cor. 1:12). Certainly, it is apparent in our unwillingness to listen to certain speakers because we might disagree with one point that they make or because they have placed an emphasis on something we don't. (Maturity teaches us to listen to speakers the same way we eat fish—we don't quit eating fish because it has bones in it. We simply lay the bones aside and enjoy the meat. So, in receiving from others, we can lay aside what isn't true to God's Word and enjoy the rest.)

Christian immaturity is also evidenced by believing the most persuasive speaker, often the last person we heard. There is a certain power of persuasion inherent in every speaker and we all must be careful to search out the truth. The opposite is true as well. Just because so-and-so is such a man of God and he said it, doesn't make it true. The Berean Christians were commended for checking out Paul (Acts 17:11).

In these days of spiritual renewal diverse voices are being heard and it is causing confusion so that people are saying, "Who can we believe?" I believe this confusion is of God. Why would He allow such a thing to happen? The answer is quite simple—to cause us to grow up!

We must *know* what we believe and why. We must know on what we base our beliefs. *It is imperative that we get into God's Word for ourselves.* We can no longer rely on others' interpretations.

If we listen to the enemy's whispers telling us that we can't or don't understand the Scriptures, we are actually denying the Holy Spirit! The Holy Spirit possesses our spirit to control the superego (conscience). When I become a Christian I possess the Holy Spirit. When I make Jesus Lord of my life the Holy Spirit possesses me. When He possesses me He can speak to me and guide me into all truth (John 16:13; I Cor. 2:10-12). The Holy Spirit is saying different things to different people in different ways, so you must learn what He is saying to *you*.

We seem to do this in other areas—what is right for me to eat and drink? where should I be spending my time? etc.—but not in the issue of womanhood.

Turning back the pages of history, we can see that as the issue of black slavery was dealt with, it brought an awareness that women also were being held back from full involvement in society. This began the fight for women's suffrage—the right to vote. For a while this seemed sufficient. Now there is a new fight on, through the women's liberation movement, with such groups as the National Organization for Women, for increased recognition and acceptance of women in all areas of society.

Is there any good in this? Yes, there is usually some good in what the enemy does, but there is such a mixture of both good and evil that it can be confusing to God's people. Various issues about which some of the advocates of women's liberation take a positive stand (such as the right to abortion on demand and the defense of homosexuality) are clearly contrary to God's Word and must be rejected by Christians.

While there is the extreme liberation position ("I am the same as a man—I can function totally independently") there is also the extreme "doormat" position ("I was born female, I'm nothing, I must be in submission. I can't function apart from a man").

How often when you have heard these extremes presented have you felt within you the response of "reject"? That's the Holy Spirit. It is His position to guide us into *all* truth and we must learn to trust the Holy Spirit within. We *can* hear from God. The only thing that would make us deaf to His voice is an attitude of rebellion. How do we know we're not in rebellion? Because our desire is to please God in everything and we are, from our hearts, praying something like "Let the words of my mouth, and the meditation of my heart, be acceptable in thy sight, O Lord, my strength, and my redeemer" (Ps. 19:14). If we're in rebellion—saying no to God—we can't trust our own feelings or the Holy Spirit within us.

If you have feelings of caution about what many are saying, get into the Word and find out what it says, trusting the Holy Spirit to make it clear to you. You don't need to fight or get angry. Just hold it in your heart, as Mary did. Be persuaded in your own conscience. We can bring our questions and concerns to Jesus and expect Him to reveal His truth to us. By studying the Word and praying we will receive true guidance.

Before You Begin

Keep in mind that we aren't just trying to gain knowledge from the Scripture for our minds, but that we desire our hearts to assimilate truth. We need to take time to let what we're learning sink in. Sometimes it helps to share it with others, or we can write it down in a journal or "spiritual diary."

Someone has very graphically stated: "Thoughts disentangle themselves when passing over the lips or through the fingertips."

Whatever method we use, we need always remember that a method is only a means to an end and if it becomes the end we've really missed it.

Regardless of methods, let's be sure to keep our minds open to all God is saying. *All* these topics are for *all* women—if you aren't in a particular circumstance, think how it would feel to be there, to better understand and support those in the Lord who *are* in that place.

> Meditate upon these things; give thyself wholly
> to them; that thy profiting may appear to all.
> (1 Tim. 4:15)

7

Understanding rhetoric—the feminine side of God—the reason we're different—biblical dignity of women—freedom from the curse—true submission

SECTION 2:

Personhood

New concepts are being explored these days and there is a struggle for words to express them. Consequently, Christian women seeking to find their way in the fullness of God's purposes for them need to be aware of what is being said. We must not be overpowered by "intellectual sounding" words or reduced to silence out of ignorance.

One phrase being much used is "the ontological approach to womanhood." The dictionary defines ontology as the branch of metaphysics dealing with the nature of being, reality or substance—that is, the base philosophy of anything. Specifically, what is being discussed, then, is the basic philosophy of the subjugation of womanhood.

In line with this, another phrase is being heard: "the androgyny of Jesus." Androgynous means having both male and female parts—whether referring to humans or plant life.

Through the use of these phrases, we can see that some proponents of women's liberation are in essence trying to make God female—or at least to emphasize a female side of God. In 1970, Betty Friedan, a NOW spokeswoman, declared the greatest debate of the decade would be whether God is male or female. Her predecessor, Emmaline Parkhurst, exhorted her followers to "Trust in God. *She* will provide."

We must learn truth. God is neither male nor female; He embodies both and is beyond both and not limited to either.

There are Scriptures revealing God as mother:

> The spirit of God hath made me, and the breath of the Almighty hath given me life. (Job 33:4)

> Hearken unto me, O house of Jacob, and all the remnant of the house of Israel, which are borne by me from the belly, which are carried from the womb: And even to your old age I am he; and even to hoar hairs will I carry you: I have made, and I will bear; even I will carry, and will deliver you. (Isa. 46:3-4)

> As one whom his mother comforteth, so will I comfort you; and ye shall be comforted in Jerusalem. (Isa. 66:13)

So also it is written, "The first MAN, Adam, BECAME A LIVING SOUL." The last Adam became a life-giving spirit. (1 Cor. 15:45 NAS)

During His earthly lifetime, Jesus referred to all three persons of the Trinity in feminine terms. He portrays the First Person as a woman seeking her lost coin:

What woman having ten pieces of silver, if she lose one piece, doth not light a candle, and sweep the house, and seek diligently till she find it? And when she hath found it, she calleth her friends and her neighbours together, saying, Rejoice with me; for I have found the piece which I had lost. Likewise, I say unto you, there is joy in the presence of the angels of God over one sinner that repenteth. (Luke 15:8-10)

He shows himself as a hen with her chicks:

O Jerusalem, Jerusalem, thou that killest the prophets, and stonest them which are sent unto thee, how often would I have gathered thy children together, even as a hen gathereth her chickens under her wings, and ye would not! (Matt. 23:37)

And the Holy Spirit is described by Jesus as giving birth:

Jesus answered, Verily, verily, I say unto thee, Except a man be born of water and of the Spirit, he cannot enter into the kingdom of God. That which is born of the flesh is flesh: and that which is born of the Spirit is spirit. Marvel not that I said unto thee, Ye must be born again. The wind bloweth where it listeth, and thou hearest the sound thereof, but canst not tell whence it cometh, and whither it goeth: so is every one that is born of the Spirit. (John 3:5-8)

Of course, He used masculine terminology as well. The point is, He was not afraid to picture God as both male and female, since He well knew that God is a Spirit (John 4:24), which includes *and transcends* human sexual dichotomy.

To consider:
Do I understand terminology being used in discussion of women today? Do I recognize that God transcends the male/female stereotypes, enabling me to accept the broadness of His character?

In Genesis 1:26-27, we see God created man and woman in His image and likeness. Father, Son, Spirit—an eternal fellowship of equals and yet they are not interchangeable. In the same way, male and female mirror this—they share the same nature and are equal but not interchangeable. God called them Adam, which means human being or ruddy.

The Bible is silent on why woman was created out of man's rib other than that she is of the same substance he is. We must be careful we don't major on things on which God is silent.

The woman was created an helpmeet which means alter ego, the other self. Help is the word *Ezer* which means *super* not *sub*ordinate, and is the same word used in Psalm 121:1-2 where it speaks of my help cometh from the Lord. It is one who can relate at every level of man's being.

The word "meet" is *Negad* and means in the presence or sight of—qualified. So it is someone who will be in his presence who is qualified. It is used in Psalm 16:8: "I have set the Lord always *before* me."

This is not limited to marriage. All women are intended to be a complement to all men. The more womanly we are, the more we can complement the male. The fact that God has made us different enables that. Women who seek to become the same as men become competitive with them, rather than complementary.

One of the ways this can be done is by input. For instance, a woman executive attending a board meeting can give input from a female point of view. The maternal instinct will allow her to see the source of employee problems and enable her to have insight regarding handling them where the men may only be concerned with the evidence of the problem. When my brother

Judson and I pastored together we frequently saw this blend of male-female point of view as beneficial to the overall management of the church.

The name-giver usually has authority over the named one, as when Adam named the animals. But he didn't name Eve *before* the Fall—he named only her gender, woman. It was when sin entered that subordination was pronounced (Gen. 3:16) and the woman was named (Gen. 3:20).

This has been interpreted in many ways, but we can at least see that subordination was pronounced as a curse because of sin and *it was limited*. The woman was ruled by her husband, not all men.

This is not what God intended life to be—not His desire. It is not a command but a statement of fact. The result of sin was what man would do in degrading women, which cannot be compared with the mutual submission which is a result of unselfish love.

We need to believe in God's perfect creation—it's good. The enemy is trying to get equality to mean sameness, to de-emphasize women. Women are not female men. This is best illustrated by the realization of the difference in the first responses of men and women. A woman's first response to anything is emotional, while a man's first response is logical. This doesn't mean women aren't logical or men aren't emotional. (An illustration of this is in section four, "Women in the Various Roles of Life.") Men and women are created equal, but not the same.

We need to understand how magnificently we're made. Then we can see the beauty of the desire to subject ourselves to one another, submit to husbands and complement all men with willingness and delight.

To consider:
In what ways have I considered myself inferior? Have I thought the ways I am different from a man to be weaknesses? Do I see myself as a woman having something to add to the quality of life of those around me, by serving as a complement or balance to men?

In biblical times, women were given a variety of freedoms, important employment, and respected status. Jesus himself showed great respect for women.

In contrast, surrounding heathen countries offered no such status. The Greeks exalted sexual gratification as the only value of women. Philosophers such as Socrates, Plato, and Aristotle warned that for wives to claim equality would disorganize the state.

In Exodus 20:12, we see divine law commanding equal honor for the mother. Genesis 24:58 illustrates Hebrew women's freedom to choose their husbands. Civil laws gave women the most possible protection (Deut. 22:16) and women were afforded social equality (Deut. 16:11-14; John 2:12, 12:3).

Women were free to appear unveiled (Gen. 12:11-14, 24:16; 1 Sam. 1:13) and had outdoor as well as indoor tasks, such as tending flocks (Gen. 29:6; Exod. 2:16) or drawing water for household guests and camels (1 Sam. 9:11; John 4:7; Gen. 24:15-20).

It was usual for women to contribute to the family income and support (Prov. 31:14-24; Acts 9:39) and to give to charity (Acts 9:39). They spun wool and made clothing (Exod. 35:26; I Sam. 2:19) and ground grain (Matt. 24:41). Besides preparing meals (Gen. 18:6; 2 Sam. 13:8; John 12:2), women also invited and received guests (Judges 4:18; 1 Sam. 25:18-31; 2 Kings 4:8-10).

In religious ceremonies and experiences, women in biblical times were also included with the men. They could take vows (Num. 6:2), offer sacrifices (Judges 13:13) and take part in religious feasts (Deut. 12:18). Women sang in choirs, choruses, and processionals of the temple (Ps. 68:25; Ezra 2:65; Neh. 7:67) and in national songs and dances (Exod. 15:20; Judges 11:34; I Sam. 18:6). They took part in religious mourning (Mark 5:38) and some were visited by angels (Gen. 16:7, 21:17, 18:9; Judges 13:3, 5, 9; Luke 1:28, 24:4).

As the Hebrew nation let themselves be influenced by the pagan peoples around them, the status of women declined. This was especially true in the court of Solomon and following kings, who turned from Hebrew morality to idolatrous practices.

> Of the nations concerning which the Lord said unto the children of Israel, Ye shall not go in to them, neither shall they come in unto you: for surely they will turn away your heart after their

gods: Solomon clave unto these in love. And he
had seven hundred wives, princesses, and
three hundred concubines: and his wives
turned away his heart. (1 Kings 11:2-3)

Thus we can see that ideas degrading women were not
from God but man. When Jesus came, He set in motion
the dynamic which had the potential to transform the
status of women. He proved what was of God and what
was of man, violating the customs of His day when they
did not truly carry out God's intention. He taught women
(Luke 8:1-3; Mark 5:38-42). He took the side of the
adulterous woman (John 8:3-11). He appeared first to
women after the resurrection (Luke 24:1-11).

We know that man and woman failed and the curse
was pronounced, but Scripture teaches that Jesus took
the curse for us in dying on the tree (Gal. 3:13). In grace
we are restored to a right position before God. Somehow
we hang on to the idea that the law was fulfilled in Christ
except for the subordination of women, that the curse
was taken by Christ, except for women. But Christ came
to break the power of sin (Rom. 5:17, 8:10-11, 19-23; Gal.
3:28; Eph. 2:14).

For Jesus, submission was an attitude, not just an
activity or action. It is not being submissive because we're
female—one can submit outwardly, while inwardly being
rebellious. Submission is not only for women but men as
well. Jesus is Lord. The very title means to be ruled by
Him, and not because I am female but because of who He
is.

The person who submits to the Lordship of Jesus Christ does so with joy because he or she recognizes He is out to do them good. Throughout Scripture husbands are told to love their wives as Christ loved the Church and Christians are admonished to be willing to lay down their lives for one another. Submission to one who loves you with this intensity certainly becomes a blessing and not a burden.

We must be certain that those who submit to us are submitting to such love and concern rather than to some kind of positional authority. If you are in a place of authority such as mother or employer a good daily prayer might be:

Heavenly Father, this day allow me to be a blessing to each of those over whom I have authority. Cause me to judge matters rather than people and grant me your specific wisdom and insight, that all correction and guidance be done in love and bring good to the person as well as the position. Let my children (my employees) as well as my family (colleagues) recognize the divine authority under which my own life is ruled. I believe you for this and thank you in advance that this day shall bring glory to your Son Jesus because of your Holy Spirit enabling me to reveal Him. Amen.

True personhood is being rightly related to God so we can be rightly related to others. It is true fulfillment of what God wants us to be.

To consider:
How have the customs of man overruled God's intentions for my personhood? How have I rebelled against God, instead of cooperating with Him to develop all that I am as a person?
Can I see that in learning true submission to God and others is the growth process for my character?
Do I know the difference between complement and control in my spirit, not just in activity?

God's intention for our bodies—true beauty—proper self-love—acceptance—God's ideas on femininity—our power to influence—caring for others—becoming a blessing

SECTION 3:

God's Purpose for Women

How wonderfully we are made, the Psalmist cries. The Lord beheld the very framework of our bodies as they were being formed while we were in the womb. Over that period of nine months' development, God's eye was upon us (Ps. 139:14-16). What care He has given to us—even to the extent that the very hairs on our heads are numbered (Matt. 10:30). Surely, since God has so involved himself in our being, we should be able to accept what He has made and rejoice in the variety of His creativeness.

Unfortunately, today, people's ideas project much guilt upon us when we don't fit their mold. Especially we see this in the area of what qualifies us to be used of God—everything from formal Bible school training to certain social positions to the shape of our figures.

Let's look for instance at this last one—we are either too fat or too thin, that is, our bodies disqualify us from being used of God. Certainly the world has placed great emphasis on a woman's measurements and there is a tremendous amount of money and time being expended on a variety of diets and exercise/body-shaping equipment. Unfortunately, this overconcern with the shape and weight of the human figure has crept into the church until in some places there is far more time spent studying how to eliminate calories from the menu than studying the Word of God.

Growing up in God demands that we see what the Bible says about our bodies, not what people say. Romans 12:1 says the body is to be presented to God as a living sacrifice. Romans 11:1 and 1 Corinthians 3:17 tell us it is to be yielded to God. It is to be full of light (Matt. 6:22), counted as dead to sin and alive to God (Rom. 6:11). We are to refuse its slavery to sin (Rom. 6:12; 1 Cor. 9:27; Col. 2:11), put to death its deeds (Rom. 8:13; 1 Cor. 6:13-20) and refuse to defile it (1 Cor. 3:17). It is to be a fit temple of the Holy Spirit (1 Cor 3:16-17, 6:13-20) and God is to be glorified in it.

From this brief view we can see where God places the emphasis. It's not what goes into the body that defiles it (Mark 7:15). God qualifies us not by size and shape, but divine usefulness comes from unity with His Holy Spirit (Zech. 4:6; 1 Cor. 2:3-4; 1 Cor. 12). We are not beseeched to be changed into any image but Christ's (2 Cor. 3:18).

But we all, with open face beholding as in a glass the glory of the Lord, are changed into the same image from glory to glory, even as by the Spirit of the Lord. (2 Cor. 3:18)

"My eye effecteth my heart," though not referring to our context, is surely a true principle. What we see does affect how we feel about something. And how we look will cause others to respond either positively or negatively. While we are not to be dependent on external beauty for self-acceptance or the response of others, outward beauty nevertheless has its place in the believer's life. We needn't be fearful of dressing in an attractive way. The Scripture bears out that lovely clothes are not anti-God. The wise lady of Proverbs 31:22 is clothed in silk and purple.

> The king's daughter is all glorious within: her clothing is of wrought gold. She shall be brought unto the king in raiment of needlework. . . . (Ps. 45:13-14)

We need to learn to recognize our assets and liabilities and find ways to turn what we may consider physical liabilities in our eyes into assets with proper clothing choices.

The latest styles are often not the best complement to us. Salespersons many times attempt to get us to purchase something merely because it's in style. Usually, you know what looks best on you. If you find that you are dressing extremely different from those about you, it's time to check up. For example, are your dresses much shorter than everyone else's?

The other extreme is to wear the latest fashion whether it looks well on you or not.

If you have a weight problem and are very full-busted, you will probably not want to wear very low necklines, which accent the bustline. The full loose look can be very complimentary to the full figure if it isn't exaggerated. Try a size smaller in these garments and leave the extra fullness to the person who is underweight. If you have ugly feet, don't accentuate them by wearing open-toed sandals just because everyone is wearing them. If you are satisfied with how you look, you will carry yourself with poise. If you dress the way someone else decrees, your walk will reveal your feeling of insecurity.

> Likewise, I want women to adorn themselves with proper clothing, modestly and discreetly, not with braided hair and gold or pearls or costly garments; but rather by means of good works, as befits women making a claim to godliness. (1 Tim. 2:9-10 NAS)

Internal beauty comes from Jesus, who is the author and finisher of our faith (Heb. 12:2). Ephesians 2:10 tells us that we are (present and continuous action) His workmanship. As we look to Him and come more and more in love with Him, Jesus becomes our love covering, and that gives us a look of security, love and care. Our

beauty is perfect through His love and comeliness which
He put on us (Ezek. 16:14).

To consider:
Have I allowed others' projections of beauty to make me
ashamed of what I wear?
How can the knowledge that God was there as I was being
formed change my self-image?
Have I been overconcerned about my physical
appearance to the detriment of my inner beauty?

There is a significance to self-love which is often
overlooked in our desire to be humble and to exalt Jesus
Christ. True humility is the awareness of who God is and
who we are in relationship to Him. It does indeed first
reveal to us our contrariness to God, but once this is
settled through the acceptance of His perfect sacrifice in
Jesus Christ, we are able to see the tremendous value God
places on each individual. Each is valuable enough to die
for—to impart His divine life to—to make a member of
His family and an inheritor equally with Jesus Christ.
(See 2 Pet. 1:4; Rom. 8:15-17.)
Therefore, we can see ourselves in this exalted position
in which Christ has placed us. We recognize that He
accepted us "just as I am, without one plea." If He has
accepted us in that way, surely we should be able to accept
ourselves, knowing that He has given us His Holy Spirit
whose regenerating power is in us to transform us to
become more like His Son, Jesus Christ (Rom. 8:29).

The great commandment begins with loving God (Matt. 22:37) and then reveals the need for self-love in order to love our neighbor (Matt. 22:39). There have been some arguments of late that loving our neighbor as ourself can only refer to provision for physical needs. However, in the parable of the good Samaritan where Jesus illustrates this command, it seems valid that the Samaritan had to accept the Jewish man as an individual beyond racial prejudice, religious practices, etc. This seems to me to show valid self-love.

When I can't accept or love myself, I am so taken up with what I'm not, I have no open channel through which to pour love to others. Lack of self-love or self-acceptance is surely inverted pride, which is just as damaging in its focus on self as boisterous overconfidence. (Some have almost been proud of having a so-called inferiority complex!) Therefore, a proper kind of love is essential. True love accepts (not just tolerates) limitations and liabilities.

For example, some are very concerned about the titles Ms., Miss and Mrs. Presumably because men are supposedly the pursuers, they have only the one title—mister—and their marital status is hidden to women. A basic attitude of inequality marks women out as Miss or Mrs. thus categorizing them immediately from the marriage point of view. The new title Ms. has been suggested for women, that they too may be incognito maritally speaking. But surely, a woman who has truly accepted herself shouldn't be concerned with this.

Acceptance should be based on what we are as persons, not whether or not we are married.

Those who haven't accepted themselves may either use or deny their marital status for acceptance. The result of reaching out of your marital status—whether single or married—is the feeling of being trapped. When you are looking for greener grass on the other side, you are missing something where you are.

To consider:
In what ways does my lack of self-acceptance limit my acceptance of others? How do I feel about my own social title and all it represents? Why?

Proverbs 23:7 says what we think is what we are. Therefore, the way we think about ourselves as well as others is not only revealing but affecting. Philippians 4:8 tells us to think on things that will make the difference.

> Finally, brethren, whatsoever things are true, whatsoever things are honest, whatsoever things are just, whatsoever things are pure, whatsoever things are lovely, whatsoever things are of good report; if there be any virtue, and if there be any praise, think on these things.

We need to set goals and work diligently toward them. If you set a goal based on what someone else thinks you should do or become, chances are great that diligence will fall by the wayside. Ask yourself three questions before setting a goal. First, what do I feel I should do? Second, what do others feel I should do? And third, and most important, what am I going to do? When you've arrived at an answer for number three, you have but one question left: when? This gives you opportunity to set both your long-range and short-range goals.

Take, for example, weight loss. It seems to be a prominent concern today. You have sixty pounds to lose and have decided that you want to lose them beginning tomorrow. How much less are you willing to eat in order to lose? If the answer is to leave off sweets and breads and between-meal snacks, you can probably count on losing three pounds a week. Consequently, your short-range goal is to lose three pounds each week and you should reward yourself for attaining it (but not with food). It's obvious if you keep your eye on your long-range goal, three pounds isn't very rewarding, so you must program yourself to realize the positive behavior modification you have affected by losing three pounds each week. This will give you faith that you can both set and attain other long- and short-range goals in the future.

The world says to think positively, but the Bible carries it a step further by giving us specific thought direction as in Philippians 4:8. Whatever is true and honest, etc., demands that instead of downgrading ourselves for being overweight, we encourage ourselves by the truth that we're doing something about it. While I believe there has been some extreme teaching on giving our weight problem to Jesus, it is true that when we focus on Him as true and love all that the previous Scripture declares, there is assurance that we're not in this battle alone. The Lord *enables* us rather than doing for us.

Ask yourself: What are my assets? Then learn to truly pray, "God grant me the serenity to accept the things I cannot change, courage to change the things I can and wisdom to know the difference."

True love trusts and appreciates. Do you trust yourself? Do you appreciate you?

"Feminine" according to the dictionary means pertaining to women, tender, modest, and gentle. Women are not female men; they are persons. The Bible has some very explicit things to say to a woman as a person. First Thessalonians 5:22 commands us to abstain from all appearance of evil. This can surely refer to the enticements to seduction which women may use. Some women deny they're seductive because their intentions are not to engage in sexual relationships. Those same women are frequently seen seducing men at social gatherings by requiring their full attention. Such seduction can become game playing and often causes hurt to those who are less qualified to play the game. For example, how many times have we been to social gatherings where all the men are gathered around one woman, laughing and delighting in her as the other women (many of them wives) stood by tolerantly being deprived of the attention that was due them? It is quite possible that the seducer in this case is actually afraid of her own femaleness and feels the need to reaffirm it to herself in this manner.

"But she that liveth in pleasure is dead while she liveth" (1 Tim. 5:6) gives direction for the emphasis of our lives and Galatians 5:16 is the antidote: "This I say then, Walk in the Spirit, and ye shall not fulfil the lust of the flesh." The true flow of love is revealed in the negatives in 1 Corinthians 13. Love thinks no evil, doesn't rush, show off, demoralize, push for selfish reasons, blow up or seduce. The virtuous woman, so exalted in the Book of Proverbs, is the woman with strength of mind and body (Prov. 12:4).

It is important as a woman to be aware of the tremendous power of influence we have. This is revealed in the Scriptures for both evil and good. Evil influence is seen in the very beginnings, as Eve influenced Adam to partake of the fruit which had been forbidden to them. Delilah manipulated Samson with her nagging in the name of love till she received the information her heart desired. Jezebel seemed to control the country through Ahab and her son. Zeresh brought the suggestion to Haman that was the beginning of the end for him.

Grandmother Lois and mother Eunice left their indelible mark for good on Timothy. Esther saved her nation by influencing King Ahasuerus. Naomi's life surely influenced Ruth to choose to go with God's people rather than remain in her own heathen country. Ruth by her humility and loveliness caused Boaz to desire her for his wife. Hannah's godly influence in Samuel's life is seen in his earliest years hearing from God. The Shunammite woman influenced her husband to make a place for Elisha. There are many more.

In Proverbs 31:10-31 we can see at least five things that the Bible describes as part of ideal womanhood: She provides food and clothing for her family (vv. 13-14). She manages her affairs efficiently (v. 15). She engages in business with prudence (v. 16). She shows compassion to the poor (v. 20). She teaches with wisdom and clarity (v. 26).

To consider:
What are my assets?
Are my goals realistic? i.e., am I dealing with something that can be changed?
Is the goal humanly reachable?
Who am I influencing? In what way?

When we have accepted ourselves as persons accepted by God and as women created by God to complement men, we are free to discover others and learn to care. In that beautiful passage in Hebrews 10:19-25, we find an account of our privileges and duties as those who now have boldness before God because of Jesus' total giving of himself for us. Not only are we responsible towards God, but we are responsible to give ourselves one to another.

Verse 24 states that we are to "consider one another to provoke unto love and to good works." The word "consider" means that we are to *thoroughly weigh one another so as to come to a full knowledge of each other.* Wuest's translation makes it very plain: "Let us constantly be giving careful attention to one another." It is the same word used in Hebrews 3:1 where it tells us to consider Christ Jesus. This is not an invitation to pry or interfere in others' lives, but a caring for them that takes into account their circumstances, infirmities, needs, trials and goals, that we might not look at them as just one of a mass. We must be aware of others' individuality and be able to encourage them in the giving of themselves in the things God has planned for their lives.

This will require that we leave extreme positions thrust upon us by the ideas of people and walk in the certainty of what God reveals to us concerning our personhood. Psalm 26:11 says: "But as for me, I will walk in mine integrity." Only then can we encourage others to do the same.

Some of us have been taught what is right and wrong by our church tradition. While we may have done what they said and refrained from what they forbade, there was not true agreement from within. To decide right and wrong is one of the most difficult dilemmas of humanity. The Christian must make such a decision with much in view. We must feel, like Paul, the responsibility that our freedom to do or not do dare not be harmful to others; yet, we must maintain the liberty that Christ has brought us into and not be "entangled again with the yoke of bondage" (Gal. 5:1). The person who is in daily communion with the Lord will not find this balance a laborious task, for the Holy Spirit within causes us to know the intent of the Bible, and that is true liberty.

In many churches in the past, lipstick on a woman was a sign of "worldliness"; they demanded the "plain-Jane" look for acceptance. Even today, there are women wearing lipstick whose traditional backgrounds intimidate them, while personal integrity of heart has set them free. They know it's not wrong, even though occasional guilt feelings may be produced from the past teaching.

Extreme positions become defenses against change, against admitting there might be some other way than ours. They cause us to be obstinate and prejudiced towards those who don't agree with us, segregating ourselves from them, and so shutting ourselves off from parts of the Body of Christ. We then become like an eye saying to the hand, "I have no need of thee" (1 Cor. 12:12-25). Thus we become unwilling to be an encouragement to those who don't do it our way.

What is our primary motive in reaching out to others? Could it be that meeting our own needs is really what we're concerned with? Do we allow ourselves to be drawn into extreme positions—or the position of whomever we're with—because we're afraid we won't be accepted? When we have accepted ourselves and are walking according to our own integrity, we can ask to be a blessing because our focus is not on what others can do for us.

Surely we have a right to have our needs met, but our needs won't get out of order unless *we* are. Our own needs can be met, but making that the purpose in a relationship usually produces wrong methods. For example, the basic drive that can not be fulfilled in the unmarried is sexual gratification. But we may receive love, touch, be cared for and secure by recognizing we are members of the Body of Christ. Whenever the focus is on blessing others, our own needs get taken care of in a right way.

God is purposing to bring us as women to the steadfast position beautifully revealed in Philippians 4:1-8. Verses 2-4 show us the need to stand fast with one another, working together and cooperating with one another so God's purposes may be accomplished. We must learn to forgive those who don't agree with us or do things the way we think best. In verse 5 we see that the outsider must be able to see our balanced life rather than extremisms. So we must stand fast toward them. The imperative of steadfastness in prayer and praise is found in verses 6 and 7. We cannot afford to eliminate one in favor of the other, but both are absolutes for our relationship with the Lord. Verse 8 shows that we must learn to rule our thoughts. Sometimes we forget that God has made us with the power to control our thought life. We want Him to do it but He has given us this ability, so, while we can't always keep a thought from coming to us, we can either eliminate it or redirect it.

These areas dealt with and kept steady in our lives will enable us to be the women God intended.

To consider:

Do I see those around me in terms of meeting my own needs?

Do I see people in their individuality or do I put them in categories?

Do I have a sense of my own integrity?

Am I a blessing to those who are members of the Body with whom I don't agree?

What is needed to bring me to a steadfast position?

Gratitude for femaleness—the role of daughter—sister—friend—breadwinner—ministry—wife—mother—setting priorities

SECTION 4:

Women in the Various Roles of Life

What is a role? It is a function or office assumed by someone. Some of these are listed in Colossians 3:17-24 in the context of putting your whole heart into whatever your role is, doing it in the name of Jesus and thanking God for the privilege.

As we have previously stated, women are not female men. We're not the same as men, not only physically, but in our responses as well. For instance, if my brother and I were both scheduled to speak at the same meeting and upon entering together we overheard someone say, "Well, I don't think either one will be any good," my immediate response would be, "They don't like us." My brother's response would be, "I wonder on what he bases that?" Now, I might regroup and think logically and my brother might upon thinking about it sense some hurt, but the first responses are different because we are male and female. God made us to complement one another, not to be the same.

To attempt to be the same is an abomination to God. He created us to be distinctly two different sexes. It doesn't have to do with what kind of clothes we wear or what we do or our likes and dislikes. It is simply a fact; we are born female.

There are varieties of people and we are to be complements to others. Let's not get involved in teaching which "pigeonholes" or types male and female are in, such as, "All women ought to be in the kitchen instead of the yard, baking instead of raking, painting pictures instead of the house." Or, "All men ought to be athletic, mechanics, carpenters, ruddy, gardeners, etc." Is it unfeminine to be aggressive or assertive? Is it feminine for men to be shy or quiet?

You are not a mistake! God knows what He is doing. Remember Moses? Don't you just know his parents were praying for a girl? (After all, every boy baby was to be killed!) But God made no mistake with Moses—or with you. You were born woman. Appreciate and utilize all that God has given as you assume your various roles.

Whatever your role, do everything as unto the Lord, knowing your reward is going to come from Him. The importance you place on each of the roles shows your priorities. Set your priorities—what's really most important?

The role of daughter: God tells us in Exodus 20:12 and again in Ephesians 6:2-3 to honor our parents. Honor means to prize, fix valuation upon. We can value our parents for their position regardless of their behavior. We can value them as those who brought forth life—ours.

> Honour thy father and mother; (which is the first commandment with promise:) That it may be well with thee, and thou mayest live long on the earth. (Eph. 6:2-3)

The role of sister: In both natural and spiritual relationships we are sisters. Romans 16:1-2 speaks of Phebe our sister, a simple affectionate term for Christian women speaking of relationship, responsibility and permanency.

The role of friend: "A man that hath friends must shew himself friendly" (Prov. 18:24). This does away with the idea that others should seek me out. We do need to reach out to others and be concerned with meeting their needs. But we are responsible for ourselves and we cannot sit back and hope for friends; we must take the initiative. The Bible has much to say about friendship and we would do well to use a concordance to study out the importance and characteristics of friends. (See Section 5 on the unmarried woman for more on friendship.)

The role of breadwinner: While unmarrieds must work for a living, if at all possible, a married woman with children in the home should not seek outside employment. Occasionally she may want to work for a few months to buy that special furniture or car that isn't provided for in the budget.

If you work to provide for your children, remember it ought to be our joy: ". . . for the children ought not to lay up for the parents, but the parents for the children" (2 Cor. 12:14). Never use this as a guilt projection in an attempt to cause appreciation from them. If you hate your job, begin looking for one that will be more stimulating. If you love your job, keep a balance; don't marry your work.

The role of ministry: Ministry simply means service. Every role you play in life can be a ministry—or none of them. Listening is a beautiful ministry (provided you don't become a human garbage can).

Women have a different approach and ways of saying things than men, even if our goals and end results are the same. There is definitely a place for women in ministry—but not as a replacement for men. Again, there is the need to be a complement to each other. Jesus received ministry from women, as did Paul and the churches. (For more on the subject of ministry, see section 9, Service in the Church.)

The role of wife: Before you were his wife, you were his sister in the Lord and you still are. The wife is the husband's partner, not property. There are some very specific principles in the Word of God for the wife. Let's take a look at them.

Wives must learn to love their husbands (Titus 2:4). Remember that love is more an action than emotion. It is the specific giving of oneself on behalf of another. This is why it must be learned. Titus 2:5 speaks of obedience, which means to put under or be subject to; the wife puts herself under by choice, not force.

First Corinthians 7:3-4 speaks of giving the husband his conjugal rights. The withholding must be mutual and only for a short time for a purpose. Proverbs 12:4 extols the virtuous woman—one who has strength of mind or body morally.

Wives are instructed in 1 Timothy 3:11 to be grave. This doesn't mean without a sense of humor but honorable, worthy of respect, not slanderous, balanced (and how we women need to learn this) and faithful in all. Titus 2:5 and 1 Timothy 5:14 show wives should be guides and workers in the home. The guide gives management and direction, as pointed out in Proverbs 31:10-31).

The role of mother: Love your children, enjoy them and appreciate them. What a need there is today to take time to really look at our kids and see them as people. (Suggested reading: *How to Live with Kids and Enjoy It*.) Teach them and train them.

> Train up a child in the way he should go: and when he is old, he will not depart from it. (Prov. 22:6)

Training means to bring to a requisite standard, as of conduct or skill, by protracted and careful instruction—specifically, to mold the character. The

Hebrew word is *chanak*, a root word meaning to narrow; from this we get the concept of initiating or disciplining. The Scripture tells us in Hebrews 5:8 that Jesus learned obedience. It's not something that happens automatically. Hebrews 12:7-11 reminds us that God chastens those whom He loves. We must realize the importance of the transfer of responsibility for actions from the parent to the child.

Since all of life consists of sow and reap, we do our children a service to teach them the value of proper sowing, thus preventing this lesson being learned through tragedy.

For instance, when your child has begun to drive the car, he must be made aware that violation of the speed law may result in financial obligation for which he, not you, is responsible. If the child is not employed, some means of work should be made available to him that he may be enabled to pay his own debt.

Two dangerous concepts are "master control" and "hypnotic training"—either trying to effect a greater sense of responsibility in the child through greater control, or using repetitions, warnings, threats, speeches and promises of reward. Freedom of thinking is not synonymous with rebellion. Allow children to explore avenues of truth without feeling they are against a truth simply because they are looking at a concept with which you disagree. *Disciplined minds discern truth*.

According to the Scripture, as a child, Jesus increased in wisdom (Luke 2:52)—not just knowledge, but an awareness of how to use His knowledge. A child is known by his doings (Prov. 20:11) and having been taught won't stumble (Prov. 4:11-13). But "a child left to himself bringeth his mother to shame" (Prov. 29:15). True teaching—a very real part of the responsibility of parenthood—is deep conviction reinforced by example.

We must learn to love our children (Titus 2:4). Maturity is needed for parenting and we do grow with the kids. We must be more concerned with their needs than ours in our dealings with them. Adults should learn to meet their own needs with adults. Then the rewards of being a parent are a plus instead of the frustration of trying to force the kids into being something to us they cannot be. (This would be like the mother who "ties her children to her apron strings" in order to meet her own security needs.)

Checklist for parents:

THINKING: Do you do it for them? What are they thinking about?

LISTENING: What are they saying? Are you hearing them?

SENSITIVITY: What aren't they saying? Why? What are their reactions to your actions (facial expressions, etc.)?

RELATIONSHIP: Do you interpret love in their relationship to you? Do you interpret love in their work only? In their play only?

IMAGINATION: Do you understand it? Or fear it? Is it

fact or fancy?

EMOTIONS: How do they handle strong emotions? How do you respond?

EXPECTATION: What do you expect from your child? Are you willing to wait?

LOVE AND CHARACTER: Do you see them bearing fruit?

SPIRITUAL STATUS: Do you know where your child is spiritually?

It may be some consolation to remember that God's patience with our children far exceeds ours. Once we have taught, trained and loved our children we have a tendency to sit back and expect perfection. It is devastating to some parents when they see their children trying some of the freeways of life and the inclination is to pick up guilt for seeming failure. Once we've done the job, we then must trust our kids to the Lord and in His faithfulness as a Father He's still with them out there on those freeways. Whatever experiences are necessary for them in order to make our teaching their life pattern, when they feel the necessity to experience the "other side," it's here that our reliance on the Promisor of Romans 8:28 is indispensable.

To consider:

Have I assumed a role without realizing the implications and responsibilities?

What are my roles in life? Which are priority and what

are my priorities in each one?
What is one definite thing I can do to better fill the responsibility where I sense a lack?

Wholeness—meeting discrimination—seeing our assets—self-appreciation—fitting in —renewal—friendship—fear of intimacy —dating—sexual desires—meeting temptation—considering marriage—myths of happiness—setting realistic goals

SECTION 5:

The Unmarried Woman

You were not created half a person. God didn't create you imperfect. You are entire, whole, complete as you are. In omniscience God created you with the capacity to join your whole life with the whole life of a man and through it have fulfillment in an entirely new dimension. But if you aren't married, *you are complete as you are*.

The problem lies in guilt feelings—a sense of "less than." People project guilt for not being married and you feel mashed down. In general, people are afraid to trust the Holy Spirit in singles and don't believe any good about them: "After all, there must be something wrong with them if they're not married."

Jesus brings good news. We are created in His own likeness and image. Though sin entered and we have fallen short of that likeness, there is a good end result. God sent the perfect Christ to regain the perfection of creation; when we appropriate His Lordship we stand perfect, whole and entire in Him (Col. 2:10).

On the positive side, recognition is coming to singles in greater employment opportunities. (Discrimination such as "married people are more settled or mature" which has kept singles from long-term or responsible jobs is being withdrawn.) Even tax benefits which had previously been only for marrieds are being opened to singles.

There are two very important things to remember: balance—between women's liberation and doormat submission—and peace—don't fight for rights, to minister, to be noticed, etc. Every time we pick up our sword, God lays His down. When I fight, I may win battles, but lose wars. When He fights, He wins them both. Fighting may get me my way for the moment but set people even more strongly against all singles. When God opens doors, people's attitudes will also be right.

We need to learn to balance out our liabilities (such as scars, guilts, fears, poverty, being unattractive, inhibitions, hate, lack of education, bad reputation, etc.) with our assets (background that has prepared you for improvement, opportunities, personality, talent, abilities, etc.). Some of our liabilities can be transformed if we care enough to put forth the effort to change them; some must be accepted.

If your lack of education is viewed as a liability, there are numerous free or inexpensive schools or educational opportunities such as evening adult education with high school and college courses which may be taken. This liability then can be corrected and you must decide on its importance.

Should you have eyesight problems and the contours of your eyes make the wearing of contact lenses impossible, you must adjust to the fact that you will always wear glasses. Look for those frames that complement your face and do not be convinced of the old fable, "Men don't make passes at women who wear glasses." Take a look around at the married women who do.

We are almost trained that seeing anything positive in our lives is to be displeasing to the Lord. One of the first roles we ever see God in is Father. Did you ever watch a father watching his son play ball? "That's my kid," he says with pride. God is the same way. "That's my kid. She's beginning to believe in herself and realize I did indeed put some good things in her. She's beginning to utilize some of her assets." It's pleasing to the Father.

But what about pride? Don't worry. There are plenty of people and situations to pop your balloons and deflate pride-filled tendencies. When we keep our motives pure, pride will never be a problem.

We need to allow ourselves some likes and dislikes in every area of our lives, knowing what we do and don't enjoy, what's meaningful to us as individuals.

Permitting ourselves to fail is imperative to life. We can learn much from each failure if we will. If we are afraid of failure, we will never try anything new, never stretch our capabilities. Putting ourselves in a rigid box not only imprisons us socially, educationally, emotionally and mentally, but also causes us to hate ourselves secretly while all the time proclaiming, "This is what I am and if you don't like it, too bad for you."

We are to love our neighbors as ourselves (Matt. 19:19). This should prompt an inventory of self-appreciation. We do have some rights—to be what we are, to do what we wish—but these are to be exercised assertively, not defensively. Being single does not make us available to everyone at their convenience. We can be willing contributors to others (by babysitting, attending the sick, giving a ride to someone without a car, assisting the church secretary on overload days) without allowing ourselves to be taken advantage of. Let's keep in mind that while we don't have any more time than marrieds, we do have more control of our time because we can eat or sleep whenever it's convenient to us. Finding balance is the key.

To consider:
Do I really believe I am complete as a single person?
In what ways have I let doubts about my wholeness limit my freedom?
What one area of my life presents the greatest problem in keeping a balance?
What is a negative in my life that I need to accept?
What is one liability that could be changed? How can I do it?

As an unmarried woman, it is natural to have problems with loneliness, unmet needs, wondering where you fit in. Just to pray about it is not the total answer for these problems. Discover the specific time patterns of your loneliness and do some preventative work. Is it at a certain time in your menstrual cycle or when you watch romantic movies or read love stories? Do you notice it especially around holidays? Learn and plan for acceptable ways of meeting your needs. Cultivate meaningful friendships. "Take a little from many, not a lot from one or two."

Limiting our friendships to our own age or marital status is to miss the richness that a broader range will bring. All the experiences of life that people have, regardless of age or marriage, add insight, humor, compassion and understanding, giving a fullness to life that we shouldn't miss.

Plan times to be with people apart from where you normally see them. If you have friends at church, arrange to be with them in other settings or if your friend is someone at your job, take time to be with them at times and places away from work. Let your relationship be developed to include more of the person than just that one aspect. It's exciting to discover different facets of each individual and to enjoy the whole person.

One tendency in seeking new friendship is to seek out the most popular person. This may be defeating because they will also be the busiest. We need to look around us and reach out beyond the one who stands out in a crowd.

Not just to "be nice" but to cultivate those who have time to be friends. In the process we may be surprised to find depths of relationships when given time and encouragement to open up.

When we are shy and tend to wait for others to ask us, we may be adding to our own loneliness. When we've never done this, it may be frightening at first—"What if I can't keep the conversation going?"—but if we are honest and make the effort, it will be met with understanding and gratefulness.

We will have different levels of friendship with various people. Some will be giving to us more than we do to them; some receive from us more than they return; with others we'll make equal exchanges, both materially and emotionally. If all our friendships are of one level, we will not be truly satisfied nor be able to mature in relationship to people.

Male and female friendship within and outside marriage is very difficult to build because our society won't let it. People are suspicious; but we must refuse to let society demand of us that which is against our integrity. When it's not sex, we know it. As C.S. Lewis wrote in *The Four Loves*: "Those who cannot conceive Friendship as a substantive love but only as a disguise or elaboration of Eros [sexual love] betray the fact that they have never had a Friend."

One reason singles are treated the way they are is because they set up to flirt instead of be friendly. There's a vast difference. The flirt is often preoccupied with touching the other person in some way and in showing off herself. The other person is not someone to conquer but someone to relate to. Today's pace is producing insecurity and a greater desire for friendship—deep, warm, interpersonal relations.

To cultivate friendship requires ridding ourselves of fears. It also requires a vision of what friendship can be. Friendship provides excellent opportunities for self-discovery and sharing in another's life.

There is much fear surrounding friendship today: fear of feelings, fear of being hurt by the severing of the relationship through a falling out or a geographical separation, fear of the cost of time and emotional energy being too great. Many are afraid of words—that is, believing that saying "I love you" is to say, "I want you sexually." There is a fear of touch such as a hug, a pat on the head, squeezing the hand or a cry on the shoulder. Jesus gave and received touch. Sudden, momentary feelings that could lead to wrong behavior must be recognized as normal human feelings—not evil. We can turn from them by an act of our will, not harboring or nurturing them.

Homophobia has come to light today. This is a fear of homosexuality. "Gay liberation" is trying to work out a theology of homosexuality with David and Jonathan, Paul and Timothy, Ruth and Naomi, even Jesus and John, causing people to fear their own feelings toward members of their own sex and seek reassurance that they are not homosexual. Where deep friendship love exists—but is void of sexual desire or behavior—the relationship is not homosexual.

To consider:
Am I consistently a "giver" or a "taker" or are my relationships balanced?
How can I act first, before loneliness gets me down?
Which ways of fighting loneliness do I now use which really make things worse?

There are a few places where, as a single person, you don't fit, such as husband and wife seminars and sweetheart banquets. Don't try to.

It is imperative to discover the Lord, spending time with Him, talking and listening, getting to know Him. Find excitement in Him who says, "Behold I will do a new thing. . . ." (Isa. 43:19). Have a love relationship with Him.

> Herein is love, not that we loved God, but that he loved us, and sent his Son to be the propitiation for our sins. (1 John 4:10)

> And we have known and believed the love that God hath to us. God is love; and he that dwelleth in love dwelleth in God, and God in him. (1 John 4:16)

Yield to Him. Yield to His Lordship.

Romans 12:2 says, "Be not conformed to this world." The Greek word means conform to another's example. This same word is used in 1 Peter 1:14: "As obedient children, not fashioning yourselves according to the former lusts in your ignorance." We are, indeed, in the world but not of it (John 17:16-17).

God's antidote to conformity is not to be a nonconformist, but to be transformed by the renewing of our minds. The Greek word is *metamorphoo*, which is to be transformed by a supernatural change, not by "mind power." Renewing simply means to make new again. We need a sane viewing of ourselves. That is, one which is seen by faith in the presence of the Lord. Apart from faith our view is distorted; apart from His presence, we are devastated.

> And be not conformed to this world: but be ye transformed by the renewing of your mind, that ye may prove what is that good, and acceptable, and perfect, will of God. For I say, through the grace given unto me, to every man that is among you, not to think of himself more highly than he ought to think; but to think soberly, according as God hath dealt to every man the measure of faith. (Rom. 12:2-3)

> There must be no competition among you, no conceit; but everybody is to be self-effacing. Always consider the other person to be better

than yourself, so that nobody thinks of his own interests first but everybody thinks of other people's interests instead. (Phil. 2:3-4 JB)

How do we make our minds new? Phillipians 2:5 says, "Let this mind be in you, which was also in Christ Jesus." Then we shall be able to prove the good, acceptable and perfect will of God (God's complete will)—that which has reached its end, needing nothing more to complete it.

To consider:
Am I free enough from fear—secure enough in God's love—to think highly of others?

Dating is different from the desire to get married. It is a vehicle for the purpose of getting acquainted. There are three things you should ask yourself if you are going to date. 1) Am I willing and capable of being a friend? 2) Is this relationship one-sided or mutual? 3) What is my true motive for accepting this date? That is, is it control (I can get him), status, "claws"? (That word means even on the first date your intent is to clutch him in such a way as to cause him to walk down the aisle with you—you want to own him. It doesn't take long in a circle of men for the description "she's out to get a husband" to be shared.) Is it what can he do for you? Will you enhance his life? If your answers are negative, don't go any further. Work on your attitude and self-esteem.

Should you discover you've accepted a date you

actually dislike just for the sake of having a date, it reveals to you the need for change. Apparently you feel inadequate either in looks or actions to be asked for a date by someone you would enjoy being with. It is necessary to do something about that because your date may feel very much different and chances of hurting him are great. Christians shouldn't use one another but bless one another.

Beware of using pressure or guilt which will set up for rejection. If you say, "I know you'll probably never want to date me again, and that's okay because no one ever does" you are doing it. Or, more subtly, "I don't know if you're going to call me again, but if you do, perhaps we could have dinner at my place." That's a good guilt projection because it won't even cost him money! Inflict no pressure to set a future date. Leave each dating time with a sense of having blessed the other person. Even if it wasn't the best time you've ever had, show genuine appreciation for your time together.

Men feel more like men when treated with respect and women feel more like women when treated like ladies. Let the blessing be for the other person.

It is important to realize the danger in dating a man who is not a Christian. If you fall in love with him you are heading for trouble. If you don't date him, you won't fall in love with him. You are better off with no man than being unequally yoked.

The Bible specifically states that a sexual relationship must be confined to marriage only. (See Heb. 13:4 and 1

Cor. 7:2-3.) Therefore, to discuss how to get around it would be rebellion against God and His plans for us. It is simply something that singles cannot indulge in. In 1 Thessalonians 5:22 we are told to abstain from all appearance of evil. So the responsibility is on us to keep ourselves. Don't put the burden of it on him. You can control the situation.

That sexual gratification is a pleasure may be true, but we cannot live in that pleasure without experiencing a deadness (1 Tim. 5:6). We are taught in Galatians 5:16 to walk in the Spirit and then we will not fulfill the lust of the flesh. If we live in the love produced by the Spirit within us, we can be established unblameable in holiness before God (1 Thess. 3:12-13). This love is expressed in 1 Corinthians 13. This love suffers long so it doesn't rush. It doesn't show off. It doesn't behave unseemingly, that is, it doesn't demoralize. It doesn't seek its own so it doesn't push for selfish reasons. It's not easily provoked, therefore it doesn't blow up. It thinks no evil so it won't seduce.

When you face sexual temptation, face the fact and tell God your feelings truthfully.

> Let us therefore come boldly unto the throne
> of grace, that we may obtain mercy, and find
> grace to help in time of need. (Heb. 4:16)

Be prepared with a knowledge of God's Word—it is a reassurance of His good intentions for us, and a protection against the temptation to think "my case is different."

> For this is the will of God, even your sanctification, that ye should abstain from fornication. (1 Thess. 4:3)

> For God hath not called us unto uncleanness, but unto holiness. (1 Thess. 4:7)

No matter how strong your desire, the temptation won't last forever. Regardless of the cost, when you choose to obey God, he will sustain and restore you. The Christ in you can deal with your struggle; by virtue of His own suffering under temptation He is able to help us in our temptations (Heb. 2:14). He is a tremendous power within you (2 Cor. 13:3-4). You do not have to give in, no matter how intense it is (1 Cor. 10:13).

Thank the Lord that when you come to the end of yourself you can learn to trust in God instead of yourself.

> But we had the sentence of death in ourselves, that we should not trust in ourselves, but in God which raiseth the dead. (2 Cor. 1:9)

Let Jesus minister to you and bring healing to your spirit. Don't dwell on the temptation or blame yourself—put it aside.

Look for relationships where you can be close, but with

less chance of being sexually attracted. Avoid knowingly putting yourself in situations which present opportunities for temptation.

To consider:
Have I allowed the world's ideas to influence my thinking on sex outside of marriage? Am I a flirt?
What is my *true* motivation for dating?
How should I handle it if someone close to me becomes caught up in the reasoning, "But we are in love"?

What about marriage? We need understanding as to why we're not married. Singles have a tendency to spiritualize their marital status using 1 Corinthians 7:34-36. But the fact is, not all unmarried women are more concerned with things of God than the married! Ask yourself, am I using my singleness now? There *is* the spiritual aspect, but many who haven't found a husband quote this while praying for the right man, using it for a Christian platitude to cover their own sense of inadequacy or guilt for not being married. Now, we do need to pray, but if we want to find someone to love, we can't just sit home and pray.

"Mine eye effecteth my heart." The first look determines whether he will ever get to know the you of you. You may say, "I know I'm not attractive, but he will just have to take me as I am." He won't!

Be realistic. Don't victimize the situation—"What can I do?" You can bring your life up in every level to what you say you want in a man. Do you want an educated man? Are you educated? Do you want an attractive man? Are you attractive? Do you want a people-loving man? Are you people-loving? What are you looking for in a husband? Did God make any like that?

Of the unmarried, twenty-five and older, most have had the opportunity toward marriage even if there was no specific proposal. There was some sort of choosing toward or away from it. You have the right to choose whether or not to marry, but the important thing is to know that you are choosing. Know why you are desiring marriage or why you are choosing singleness. Be honest about yourself.

What are your reasons for wanting to marry? The most common are: "I'm so tired of working, I want someone to support me," sexual gratification, and "I want a man of my own, someone I can be proud of." Supposing you marry for any of those motives and six months later your husband has an accident. He can no longer work for a living, it prevents sexual activity and it mars his face or severs an arm or leg so there's no longer pride of ownership. What happens to your marriage?

Until I become aware of God's pattern and planning—until I see myself not only able but willing to bring everything I am educationally, environmentally, psychologically and physically—until I am willing to bring all that into the life of a man to beautify him and benefit him and complement him so the two of us can become one—I am unprepared for marriage.

So you must decide why you wish to marry. Do you want to be a blessing? God has permitted everything in your life, even the negatives that He might bring beauty.

Taking all that makes you you, can you approach marriage with the attitude of bringing your self as a complete individual to be melded into one by God with another complete individual? Then you are ready to begin to approach marriage.

God wants to be the central point of every marriage. He wants the two of you together with everything He created in each of you to be to the glory and honor of God almighty. That's the home that's in divine order which the world is seeking to see. It's God's pattern.

To consider:

At which points in my life have I chosen towards marriage or singleness? Did I realize I was making choices?

Have I thought of marriage as a total giving of a whole person, or more as a way of making up for a lack in myself?

Have I been trying to "spiritualize my singleness"?

Is marriage really what I want?

What are my reasons for desiring marriage?

What am I doing to prepare myself for it?

Singles often believe the myth that they will be safe if they settle down and organize their lives around an approved set of goals such as marriage, children, etc.

They think that if married they will be less restless and it will promote emotional security. This includes the idea that their sex life will be safe and their future manageable. The results of this myth will be few or no new directions in your life, you will be less curious about the world and become repetitive, change will always be threatening, interest in that area will one day wane and you will face the future without real challenge.

The need is for short-range and long-range goals that are realistic for you. In order to set reachable goals, you must first face your actual responsibilities—making a living, indebtedness, etc.—then set goals accordingly.

Here are some areas to think about and questions to help in setting goals:

FINANCES: Are you paying your tithe? bills? spending wisely?

JOB: Is it rewarding? progressive? Are you educated for the job you want?

HOME: Have you made it home? Do you like it? Do you enjoy it? Do your kids? friends?

FRIENDS: Is it mutual or one-sided? Do you pursue?

MARRIAGE: Why? possession, pride of ownership, freedom from work, sexual fulfillment, companionship? Or are you capable of being a complement to him?

PLEASURE: Can you budget time? Discover fun, develop creativity, talent perhaps through classes.

SPIRITUAL MATURITY: Discover the areas He is

ready to deal with and begin working on them. Study—pray—do; don't over-do.

Wise goals will keep us from living in fantasies or illusions. Psychiatrists know that serious depression and self-hate are more often than not the results of extreme disillusionment, and can even lead to suicide. They tell us that disillusionment is not possible without fantasy.

Four of the most common and destructive illusions in our society are: Shangri-la—that is, the idea that somewhere there's a paradise on earth which is problem-free; the belief that money can buy inner peace; the idea that love eliminates all difficulties; the myth that marriage will provide all we lack.

Real maturity is the process of making decisions and charting your course, learning to accept teaching and to appropriate the lessons of life, and learning to relate God's Word to your total life.

To consider:
Are my goals only long-range or only short-range? Are they realistic? What illusions do I find hard to let go of?

Mutual submission—headship—value of submission—choosing from the heart—a strong but submissive wife—unity—marital sex—being used for a blessing

SECTION 6:

Balanced Headship
in Marriage

You don't have to submit to anyone but Jesus to go to heaven. But if you want to progress—to grow—submission must become a part of your life. (I believe we can stop our growth anywhere along the line without penalty. For instance, you can be saved, baptized in water, baptized in the Spirit and endure till Jesus comes. Those experiences and their effect won't be taken away from you, but the joy of them will be lost.)

If you have chosen to become a wife (see section 5 for discussion on reasons for marrying) your submission will be in the context of marriage. Paul calls for mutual submission within the family and the church.

> There is neither Jew nor Greek, there is neither bond nor free, there is neither male nor female: for ye are all one in Christ Jesus. (Gal. 3:28)

Submitting yourselves one to another in the
fear of God. (Eph. 5:21)

There is not superiority or inferiority in God's plan for
men and women.

Let's interpret exegetically the Scripture regarding
headship. In both Hebrew and Greek society, the wife
was under the "power" of her husband; he was expected
to "rule" over his wife. In the New Testament, Paul says
the wife has "power" or authority over her husband's
body, just as he has power over her body.

The wife hath not power of her own body, but
the husband: and likewise also the husband
hath not power of his own body, but the wife.
(1 Cor. 7:4)

Scripture says wives are to be subject to their husbands,
but it has already said they are to be subject to one
another. The husband is told not to rule over her but to
give himself in (agape) love to her. This is not romantic
love, but the love which caused Jesus to serve us and to
give His life for us.

Submitting yourselves one to another in the
fear of God. Wives, submit yourselves unto
your own husbands, as unto the Lord. For the
husband is the head of the wife, even as Christ

is the head of the church: and he is the saviour of the body. Therefore as the church is subject unto Christ, so let the wives be to their own husbands in every thing. Husbands, love your wives, even as Christ also loved the church, and gave himself for it; That he might sanctify and cleanse it with the washing of water by the word, That he might present it to himself a glorious church, not having spot, or wrinkle, or any such thing; but that it should be holy and without blemish. So ought men to love their wives as their own bodies. He that loveth his wife loveth himself. (Eph. 5:21-28)

The submission Paul is speaking of here is to bring glory to God's name, to please Him, knowing it will be well with you. This is submission to love's headship—not domination. Jesus is the head of the Church and as a Shepherd He is leading. Rulership produces strife and discord.

This is explained in 1 Corinthians 11:3.

But I would have you know, that the head of every man is Christ: and the head of the woman is the man: and the head of Christ is God.

Jesus is at the right hand of God as one with Him, with mutual love, respect and fellowship between them. (It is difficult to imagine the father authoritatively ordering

Jesus around or with a lack of consideration for Him.) The head of man is Christ. How a man sees Christ is how he sets himself in headship. That is, if he sees Christ as dominating, he sets himself up as a dictator issuing orders instead of fellowshiping.

One reason for the extreme teaching sometimes called "doormat submission" may be because if we're given an inch we take a mile! So God has allowed this teaching to come in order that we might learn to be quiet in spirit, teachable, consistent in living.

It's not that women have no right to be heard. We do—but let's learn with all submission so we have something valuable when we are to contribute.

God is working in us to bring us into the position of His bride. Some things between a bride and groom are sacred—not only secret, but of special meaning just to them—we don't tell everyone. We must learn to know Him and learn that everything we receive from God is not necessarily to be shared, so that men can learn to trust us as sisters.

To consider:
Have I forgiven my husband for the times he has "ruled" rather than led?
Am I able to see myself in God's order and purpose, or do parts of me rebel at the idea of submission? Can I keep some things to myself?
What kind of "picture" of Christ and the Church does my marriage make?

There is a difference between being forced to do something and choosing to do it. Colossians 3:18—"Wives, submit yourselves unto your *own* husbands, as it is fit in the Lord,"—has been pulled out of context and used as a whip by some. But the whole chapter speaks of mutual love, peace and thankfulness, "And whatsoever ye do, do it heartily, as to the Lord, and not unto men" (Col. 3:23).

We can no longer "function without unction." That is, we can't do things because others tell us that is the way it should be done. Instead, all that we do should be out of the working of God's Holy Spirit in our hearts giving us the desire and the ability to please Him.

Let's not pick up every "new" set of formulas for successful living that comes along. We need to stop being gimmick-centered and viewers of the spectacular and become Christ-centered—"that I may please Him." Get in the Word and make it work.

There are several examples of balanced headship in the Scriptures. (Read about the Shunammite woman in 2 Kings 4:8-37 and 8:1-16, for example.) But let us look at Abigail as found in 1 Samuel 25.

We find a description in verse 3; Abigail was beautiful and of good understanding while Nabal, her husband, whose very name means fool, was churlish and evil in his doings.

The situation in verses 14-17 reveals the servants of Nabal placing the responsibility on Abigail for the situation Nabal has created. The servants use her and she uses them. This is a good illustration of body ministry—cooperating together. Behind her actions is the motivation to save Nabal and she devises and carries out her plan without telling him at that particular time (vv. 18-19). Her submission and reverence are shown and she identifies herself with Nabal as one (vv. 23-24).

She gives advice to David (vv. 28-35) and he blesses her for it and receives it. Thus Nabal is spared his life and David is spared from avenging himself. We see her sensitivity in verses 36-37. She knows timing is important. Nabal is too drunk to converse. At the right time she tells him but he is unrepentant when he is sober.

The result (vv. 39-42) is that Nabal is smitten by the Lord and dies. Abigail becomes David's wife by choice instead of as a captive.

As a helpmeet you are one who can relate at every level of your man's being—spiritual, social, physical, intellectual and emotional. You are not to exceed or even match but relate. No one has the effect on your husband that you do—to his spirit, sensitivity; to his soul, sharing all you know and learn; to his body, "to have and to hold." It is necessary to seek freedom from fears, resentments and inhibitions so as not to deny your husband.

A true helpmeet will not be attacking the weak places of her partner, things that he cannot or will not change, such as physical traits or the vocation he has chosen, nor will she de-throne him by putting him down in front of the children or friends, speaking of his inabilities, etc.

How important it is to remember you are heirs together of the grace of life (1 Pet. 3:7).

God desires sex to be a means to unite and delight. The motivation behind a man's sex drive, however, may certainly be more than love, the desire for children, etc. Sometimes tension will cause him to seek sexual satisfaction, or the excitement of change, such as being on vacation. Knowing this can help a wife to be more receptive when "romance" doesn't seem to be apparent.

Sex was never intended to be used as a tool of control. It's not a reward for gifts or for permission to go somewhere. You are uniting your lives in the most intimate manner God has allowed in creation. Each belongs to the other.

There is an overemphasis on unmet needs in this area and a minimizing of them in other important areas. Keep your perspective straight. Don't try to find in the bedroom what can only be found in the prayer room. You are not being used when you are a complement to your husband. You took the vow "to have and to hold." Can you appreciate the beauty of being possessed and held and sharing in the blending of lives—including the body?

Do you feel like you are being used? Be grateful. Isn't that what you've been asking God to do? "Use me, Lord." God puts us into situations and places to be useful. Do you want to be useful or important? Do you want to be useful only outside your home, with people you don't know? Do you want to be useful, but only when you decide to be so?

Be a blend, a blessing, a complement to every life you touch. With this motivation you won't say, "Do I have to?" but, "Lord, I need grace." "Whoso findeth a wife findeth a good thing, and obtaineth favour of the Lord" (Prov. 18:22). Can we pray, "Make me a blessing"?

To consider:
Do I realize that God has me in the situation I need to be in, and He has everything under control? Why am I still resentful at times?
In what parts of my role as wife am I a blessing? In which am I not a blessing?

Healing memories—forgiveness—why God hates divorce—remarriage—feeling rejected—finding new headship—taking only what's right—meeting needs—facing responsibility—lessons from Scripture—fighting loneliness—financial control

SECTION 7:

The Role of Divorcee

The divorce category is the least accepted of all the unmarried. Remarriage is the big issue. If you are looking for a loophole, you can find it—but then you must try to place the blame. However, there is rarely an innocent party. Loved, happy, well-adjusted mates usually don't leave home! So we must admit our own failure in the marriage and recognize our own guilt in it.

Sometimes it is difficult for us to face this reality. But if we will get into the presence of God and ask Him to show us where we were wrong, He will. As He reveals we can be forgiven, cleansed, healed and freed.

It is God's will that two should remain one. Anything less than this is missing the mark, which is sin. Therefore, all divorce is sin. Because we have missed the mark we have sinned, but it is not the unpardonable sin. Confess it, be forgiven and cleansed. This frees us from the guilt of divorce.

Perhaps the reason you haven't forgiven yourself is that you haven't come to Jesus in confession. If you're still blaming your husband for the divorce, you aren't released.

Perhaps you have gone to people for pity. The benefits of this are short-lived. When the pity party ends, you are alone with your guilt. According to Matthew 6:14-15 and Mark 11:25, forgiveness is mandatory. One reason you can't forgive your ex-husband is because you can't forgive yourself. Sometimes we don't know we have an unforgiving spirit. If you never want to see him again, you need to! Verbally say to the Lord, "I forgive so-and-so." Say it till your heart agrees with your mouth. You must forgive. There's no option.

Jesus forgave when He was on the cross suffering physical pain and mental anguish, feeling deserted, rejected by God himself. Stephen forgave as the stones hit, causing physical death. "And forgive us our debts *as* we forgive our debtors." Forgiveness is release, from the bondage of guilt, from the crippling sense of failure and depression, from the inability to start a new life. It is release first to the forgiver and then to the forgiven.

Verses often quoted and used to bring condemnation to divorcees are Matthew 5:31, Luke 16:18, Mark 10:9, Romans 7:2 and 1 Corinthians 7:10-11. What we don't realize is that these verses were written for the advantage of women. Christ taught not a law but attitudes. He didn't teach don't do this or that but taught don't *want* to do it.

Historically, when a man got tired of his wife as she

became older, he just threw her out of the house and brought someone else in. So Moses gave a writ of divorcement so the wife could be free to marry someone else. This was the law of Moses.

Jesus showed this was because of their hardness of heart. They had no right attitude at all. Moses set this law up to give some form of government and protection for the ladies. Women didn't have the right to divorce but men did. The attitude of this whole thing was adulterous. They were ignoring what God said marriage was and were dealing with it from the sensual level. All they wanted was someone more exciting and when that waned they were willing to forget God and throw it off and move toward the desire of the flesh. That's adultery!

The loose attitude of marrying with the idea "if it works, it works, and if it doesn't, it doesn't" is the attitude of the unbeliever. The Lord said, that's not true of my people. God said, my people will see marriage as sacred, realizing there will be hard places, but the two shall become one. If any other attitude is taken, it's adulterous.

So Jesus gave us a measuring stick. God sees the two of you as one. Start from where you are. If you are loosed, don't seek to start it all over. When the other remarries, he's dead to you as far as marriage is concerned (Deut. 24:4).

What about remarriage? Are you under law? Whatsoever is not of faith is sin. If you can't remarry by faith—don't. But you must know for yourself. Don't let people put guilt on you and don't try to find a book to convince you. Go on in Christ from this point on. If you go to the pastor and say, "Can I?" what can he do but read specific Scriptures to you? This is an area we make rigid rules about and others we minimize. For instance, Revelation 21:8 says all liars shall have their part in the lake which burns with fire. Have you ever lied? Yes, but when you confessed it, it was cleansed.

Did it ever occur to you that God could have stopped the divorce? But perhaps we needed to learn some things. We come the easiest route we will come. No one has your answer but your Lord. Don't struggle with the problem of remarriage until you need to. What's behind you is behind you. Leave that thing.

We must be careful not to become judgmental of others and not to judge ourselves except in the Lord. Remarriage should come under the considerations for marriage—Christians to Christians only. (Note: A good study of remarriage is *Divorce and Remarriage* by Guy Duty, published by Bethany Fellowship.)

So often we feel that people don't like us because we're divorced. But I wonder, do we set ourselves up for rejection? We mope. A simple question such as, "Are you married?" can be that little sore spot in us and down we go, low. Nobody wants to be around that. People, most of the time, don't choose against you because you're divorced but because of how you act.

Divorcees have said, "The pastor won't let me teach because I'm divorced." But possibly you weren't chosen to be a teacher because you go up and down in moods, or you're not faithful. Maybe somebody said something and you read into it, or perhaps the fruit of the Spirit is missing in your life. We're the touchiest of all groups. We're more vulnerable because we're living failures. But every person in Christ had to come to the position of "I am a living failure" in order to receive Him. "God be merciful to me a sinner" is the only route *anyone* can come.

Now we're born again, re-created. Once we receive, we're no different from others. We're liberated. We can drink from the implanted spring of living water (John 7:37-38).

To consider:
Do I really believe all is forgiven?
Have I forgiven my ex-husband for what he wasn't as well as what he was?
What is my personal sore spot?

There is a clean-up going on in the church now, but the enemy uses this to throw guilt at us. And when he does there is always a nugget of truth in it. There is no truth in his motivation towards us. He uses truth to beat us. Just when we want to pray, he comes with the truth. "Yes, but . . . you did . . . didn't do . . . that. You wouldn't submit, etc." There is a renewed emphasis on order in the home and family—headship. The enemy uses this as a club on you. He will take a reality and divert it to a counterfeit. Don't be ignorant of his devices. He keeps saying the same thing to us because it works. We have to grow up.

Headship speaks of authority. When the man steps out the woman must step in. You must learn the position of man and woman and be both. Over the children you exert headship and authority—but don't try to be masculine. Do fill the position. Become the priest in the home, representing God to the children and the children to God. Ask for wisdom. Deal with God, not the problem. The Lord ministers through you to them.

Women submit in *spiritual* headship under their pastor, not under headship of any male. You are on your own. You submit to your pastor only on spiritual things such as help with doctrine, prayer for you, etc. The pastor is not over you in other matters.

Don't usurp some other woman's husband's time. When we take a pastor's time on other matters, even though sex is not involved, we are usurping. We just want attention. Ministers' wives have a problem with us because we're so needy we take time for counsel, etc., that he should have for his own family. *God says you're strong enough to take this*, or He wouldn't have permitted it. You are complete in Him (Col. 2:10).

Certainly we can receive advice from others in any area we are unsure of—buying a car, etc. But we must be careful that we are getting an opinion and not that we are asking someone to make the decision for us or causing them to spend time with us to the detriment of other responsibilities.

If you're married don't seek to be loosed, if you're loosed don't seek to be married is the advice given in

1 Corinthians 7:27. Accept your position and status. Accept what you are and move into it. Divorce is a matrimonial state, not a way of life—unless you make it that way. You're not so uniquely different; the only thing different is your marital status.

We cannot say, "I have the same sexual needs and drives as before and I'll meet them any way I can." We have the responsibility to say, "Well, that's one area that's out." It's only a big deal if we focus on it all the time.

We must take care of ourselves. Submitting to one another doesn't mean telling everybody everything. Learn, however, to trust Christ in one another, as well as to submit in ideas, love, ego, etc.

Failure can be release. Once you've utterly failed, what pride is left? Now rise in prayer as Paul did.

> I can do all things through Christ which strengtheneth me. (Phil. 4:13)

This is great freedom. We can take our way or His way. It is in the doing that I'm strengthened. It strengthens me to rule my thoughts, to minister, to be a priest in my home. Every time we take an authoritative stand in our homes we're stronger. It will be easier next time. Every time we take a position of love when we want to flare out in anger, we're stronger.

To consider:
Do I know when to seek help and when to trust God alone

for my help?
Am I afraid of responsibility?

Divorcees can learn from Hagar, whose story is told in Genesis 21:14-21. She was a concubine, but Abraham took her assuming responsibility for her and for the son which he had by her—so she is like a divorcee.

Hagar was put out and wandered in the wilderness. Do you remember the feeling when you found out you were not necessary, not needed any more? You were given the responsibility of the child and bread and water (an amount of money) and told to go on your way.

You didn't know what to do or how to do it. When Hagar's water was gone, she cast her son under a bush and gave up. In a subtle way, we take this stand. It's not literal death, but when the money is gone and the kids come to hard places in their lives (controversial points), we have the tendency to say the same thing. "I just don't want to see him throw himself to the dogs," "I don't want to see her become what she's headed for," "I just can't look."

Hagar wept and it indicates she prayed. God heard the voice of the child. The child sees his mother and knows they have nothing going for them, he sees the water's gone, he sees the defeat and despair on her face. Apparently he had some background training, because he called to God.

Fear is our greatest enemy. God speaks, "Arise!" Don't just sit there and cry. That our children have called on God should encourage us. It's hard to do, even after God speaks to us. Get up from lying down and feeling nothing, from self-pity, from fear of motivation and lack of it.

"Get the child up." Speak encouragingly to your kids. "Hold him in thine hand." Keep him there. We have the responsibility to raise him whether it looks "heavy" or not. You have an eternal life in your hands.

God opened her eyes and she saw—not another sum of money, but the source of it—the Supplier. God is the source of life and living. He is Lord of the income and the outcome. He is Lord of health and kids.

Then she saw her responsibility was to go to the well, fill the bottle and give it to the child. So find the source. He is Lord. You don't have to worry about "what if's." Face each thing as it comes—with Him.

To consider:
Do I think it's no use to care?
Can I thank God that even in this He's left an example of what to do?
What am I imagining that makes me afraid?
Can I lay aside the "what's if's" and trust God?

In raising children the most important thing is attitude. If we give the impression "Dad's no good," or "Poor me," it can create in a boy self-hatred and it could be setting up a girl for sexual difficulties and bad heterosexual relationships.

If you have only weekend visitation periods with them,

the best thing to do is just to love them. You can't do a whole lot of instructing, etc. on weekends. Don't pump them about the other parent. Remember you cannot be God to your children—you can't have all the answers. (Note: Read *How to Live With Kids and Enjoy It*, by Iverna Tompkins, published by Logos International.)

To consider:
Have I been guilty of pointing out all the bad parts of the children's father to them?
Can I begin to focus their attention on the good things?
How can I help my kids to see that the divorce was not their fault?

There is a caution in some married ladies that you are after their husbands. Are you after her husband's attention? You may not be trying to split the home, but just enjoying his attentiveness. But we have no right to monopolize his attention for the whole evening. It is our obligation to set the home at ease by making the effort to create a tension-free atmosphere. It is up to us to use discretion so that we don't take more than we should from the husband. We must assume responsibility for the relationship.

We can be careful not to allow ourselves to exclude any of the family for any length of time in conversation. We certainly don't need to talk about our problems, or try to make a confidant of the husband. Encouraging others, instead of looking to them to help us and like us, is the better way. Even if the wife is in the kitchen and we are in the living room with the husband, keep her included in the conversation. Bless the home where you visit.

As we have said in other chapters, you are responsible not to put yourself in a position to tantalize yourself. Turn your eyes and ears to other things to divert your attention. You set the limitations. Don't try to meet all your needs with one person. "Remember, take a little bit from a lot, not a lot from a few."

Jesus assumes the responsibility for us, helping us as a husband—providing, guiding—but it has nothing to do with the carnal nature. We can't try to appropriate Him in our carnal nature. It's enmity with God. We're given the ability and capacity for sexual appetite within the bonds of marriage. We may not satisfy this outside the bonds of marriage whether we like it or not. Engaging in sexual intercourse outside of marriage is sin—enmity against God.

We have many appetites and they aren't sin—food, sex, the need to be touched, etc. We are capable of living with an unsatisfied area, but not with all areas unsatisfied. Here is an area we can't have—just X it out. But there are other areas we *may* have, so we can meet our needs in them. Find pleasure, love from friends and family, etc. We can meet some needs in very acceptable ways.

Sometimes we are more prone for sexual activity. Learn to divert your attention. Protect yourself from temptation. When you're strong those things don't bother you, but when you're weak guard yourself.

To consider:
Do I somehow think I am less of a woman because I can no longer have sexual relations?
How can I satisfy my desire to be appreciated and loved?

If you are lonely—decide why you are lonely. Is it because you are not with people, or because you are sitting around nursing some memories? Did something just happen that reminded you of something in the past? When you realize why, you can deal with the problem specifically, as it really is.

If you are not pursued and don't ask someone to come over because they didn't initiate the invitation, that's self-pity. No one wants to spend time with you because they feel sorry for you. Instead, cultivate an action pleasing to someone—have a dinner party, think of fun places to go. While this can be just a palliative, it can also be a great time—depending on what you make it. If your attitude is, "Here's a way we can have a good time," that's what it will be.

Make an offer they can't refuse. Make as many calls as are necessary to come up with someone. Some are "all or nothing at all" people. If you are going to be that way, you will be lonely.

To consider:
Does it hurt my pride to have to make my own good time?

How can I become more realistic?
What activity might someone I'd like to know enjoy doing with me?
Have I somehow assumed I don't deserve to have a good time?

Finances are often a problem for divorcees. If you need to, consolidate your debts—but don't buy anything else on time until your consolidation debt is paid. Get your finances in order. When you get out of debt, promise yourself you will stay free.

Budget wisely. Set realistic goals for yourself. Budget for some fun, too! Buy only one thing at a time and pay when things are due. Be a good steward and remember, you don't give God ten percent, He gives you ninety. Since all we have is from Him, we must take a responsible position concerning what we do with it. We need to be good managers of what God has entrusted to us.

To consider:
How do my finances reflect my inner self?
Are they orderly or confused?
Where are my priorities?

Helping people understand—hope within grief—nine steps of grief—guidelines for widows—learning from three widows (love and usefulness)—learning from a widow (willingness to receive)

SECTION 8:

The Role of Widowhood

Widows are the most socially accepted of all unmarried women, but they are just as much alone and not necessarily having their needs met either, because our culture doesn't know how to deal with death.

People don't always know how to talk with widows. So as a widow, it's your responsibility to teach people how to relate to you. Learn to help others see your acceptance of death. As you discuss with them your loss of a loved one, they'll be able to converse without fear of offending you.

One of the difficulties we face is that death is so permanent, we don't know how to grasp it. Time, of course, causes us to eventually be able to accept this reality—but at first we go through the shock and panic of grief. The unknown portion of death raises all kinds of questions. Is there life after death? What is it like? Can they see us? The unknown often strikes fear into our hearts, but God in His great mercy doesn't want us to fear death. We have a hope.

> But I would not have you to be ignorant,
> brethren, concerning them which are asleep,
> that ye sorrow not, even as others which have
> no hope. For if we believe that Jesus died and
> rose again, even so them also which sleep in
> Jesus will God bring with him. For this we say
> unto you by the word of the Lord, that we
> which are alive and remain unto the coming of
> the Lord shall not prevent them which are
> asleep. For the Lord himself shall descend
> from heaven with a shout, with the voice of the
> archangel, and with the trump of God: and the
> dead in Christ shall rise first: Then we which
> are alive and remain shall be caught up
> together with them in the clouds, to meet the
> Lord in the air: and so shall we ever be with the
> Lord. Wherefore comfort one another with
> these words. (1 Thess. 4:13-18)

God has not given us a spirit of fear. As we begin to
understand His provisions and care, His love conquers
our fear.

Heaven's attitude toward death is "They are coming
home." We rejoice for them, but we mourn our loss.
Grief is not wrong. But it is wrong to stay in it. Grief is a
beautiful vehicle God has given us to get us from one
place to another. It is intense emotional suffering—not

limited to death but may be caused by any loss, sorrow, etc.

There are nine steps in grief: 1) The state of shock. 2) The expression of grief. Crying is most normal, but some just need to be alone. 3) Then there is the feeling of depression and great loneliness. 4) Physical symptoms may appear. 5) Panic! Where? How? What? (Don't tell a person not to feel this way.)

6) Guilt. This is subtle—i.e., "It must have been something I did." And of course this is coupled with the inability to set things right. Our subconscious works with the sensory capacity (touch, taste, smell, emotion, etc.). It is like a Polaroid camera attached to a computer. It takes instant pictures and files the picture in us. It just sits there, but if any event of taste, touch, etc., is similar enough, the minute it happens the computer pulls that picture and matches it and we are reminded of that experience. Then we have guilt feelings and don't even know why.

Maybe somewhere along the line you wished the other person dead. So now it says, "You wanted it, you got it." Remember, Jesus has the key to death and hell (Rev. 1:18). We can't change what God's providence is determined to accomplish. We cannot send someone to death or hell—and the devil can't either!

What about someone you're not sure was a Christian? If that man was ever going to be a Christian, he was a Christian when he died. God's grace and mercy are everlasting. In His foreknowledge, if God knew there was ever a chance for this person to be saved, He's got the key to death and He could have prevented that death. He will wait and wait until the person will surrender to Him.

This is not to give false hope, but we simply don't know what took place in his last few moments of life. What comfort is there in this? To release you from thinking, "If only he could have attended this class—if only I could have gotten him to that man of God." No, God is bigger than that. The only ones who are gone are the ones God ordains to be gone. The devil has no power over life and death. God's mercy is open to all. His provision has been made. The Lord knows them who are His. Rest. It's in His hands. "But if only I'd known, I'd have done things so differently." That's not true—you would have done exactly what you did, when you did it.

7) Hostility and resentment rise up against God and everyone. "God, there was no reason for him to die. It was a happy marriage. Why?" He is Lord. We can trust Him; nothing is out of His control. God is bigger than all circumstances. God plans just the right time. My limited knowledge wants to keep him here. We don't know why. Leave it there. Be released. God's reason—it was good for him and good for you. That's a word of faith. Speak it.

8) You feel unable to return to your usual activities. You want to leave the state or your church or your job. "If only I didn't have to see people we both knew together."

The amazing thing is that you can go to bed on step 8 and wake up on step 9! 9) Hope is born again and we regroup ourselves. We get up and get on with the program, although it's not easy.

We don't have to spend any length of time on any one of these steps. Some refuse to leave certain of these steps ("Yes, but . . . ."). God has made us so that we can bear pain, sorrow and loss. Attempt to get over grief quickly.

> Thou hast turned for me my mourning into dancing: thou hast put off my sackcloth, and girded me with gladness. (Ps. 30:11)

God's promise to you is Psalm 146:9, ". . . he relieveth the fatherless and widow."

Scripture teaches widows not to be tattlers or busy-bodies (1 Tim. 5:13)—but to be pray-ers (Luke 18:1-8) and givers (Luke 21:2-4). Sometimes we think widows should have some special care from the church. But the Scriptures reveal that the most that was given to them was food and clothing (and that was in a time when they had no social security or pensions). Certainly, love is going to be concerned about any member of the body who is truly in want. Many times, however, we are expecting intervention that we have no right to.

Your goals and plans died with your husband. Now the widow must form new goals and plans. God trusts you and He's given you this responsibility. There is a purpose in your being left, but you are in no condition to know it. So much of our understanding is in retrospect. We look back and say, "Oh, that's why." As you continue to walk with the Lord,

He will continue to unfold His plans and purposes step by step, just as He did when your mate was alive. So let love have its perfect work.

To consider:
What step of grief was hardest for me? Have I left it behind?
Do I see the uselessness and damage of my feelings of guilt? How should I handle those thoughts?
Do I really believe I am still a whole person, or have I assumed I'm worth less now that my husband is gone? How must my goals be changed to face reality?

In the book of Ruth, three widows are portrayed from whom we can learn.

The first widow is Orpah. Her name means youthful. Immaturity is characterized by self-centeredness. She is given the opportunity to concern herself with herself by going back to the old things. The world says, "Now that you're set free and alone, you need to meet your needs." The defense of this is, "I'm young, I have lots of needs, so I must meet them the only way I know how." This is taking the easiest route out and there is no strength in that—except you will find the majority going that way and the only strength will be in staying in a large group. In pursuing self-centeredness, self-pity and self-goals, are you setting aside your responsibility to your children, your friends, etc.?

Naomi is grief-filled over her husband, who was less

spiritual, and her sons, who married heathen wives, but she shared her God, her home and her sons. We see a selfless nature. She desired to give everything she could to the girls. She doesn't let them come with her because of self-pity, but asks them to take inventory. "Why do you want to come along?"

Older widows can share with the younger. Ask them, "What are you looking for? What is it you want?" Younger widows need to be able to receive.

Naomi had selfless love. She followed her husband under headship to a heathen land. When she became head, she made her decision to go back to God's way. She was willing to get into the full swing of what God had planned for their lives. She wanted the girls to go all the way into God, knowing His way and being satisfied with it.

Ruth is young and beautiful, but her concern was for some deeper things than she knew she possessed. Her name means friend. She had a concept of what friendship was all about and knew it was give and take. She had to receive some things she didn't possess. She didn't pretend to be all-wise or know Naomi's God. She was what she was.

When opportunity was afforded her for some counsel, advice, guidance and to know the true and living God, Ruth decided to become the person God wanted her to become. She saw in Naomi all the attributes and beauty she wanted in her own life. ("Be ye followers of me, even as I also am of Christ" in 1 Corinthians 11:1 gives the same instruction.) We see in someone a good pattern; when we find out how they get that way, we choose to go the same way. In the balance of the Word, that's the body ministering together.

Orpah said, in effect, "I want my own life. Get off my back. I'll live for myself." Of the other two, the older said, "I like having you around. You can do the things for me I can't do for myself." The younger said, "I like being around you because you're feeding some things into me I can't get by myself." That's the body working together. It brings usefulness into focus and gives a genuine concept of what it's all about.

Don't get so ethereal—"I don't want to just set the table," "I don't want to go out here twelve miles and minister to a chronic crank," "I want to do something great for you." The Lord says, "Go where I send you. Pray for this one in the market, this time. Smile this time. Encourage another. Pat her on the head."

To consider:
Which widow do you identify with? Do you really want to be useful?

Beware of daydreaming—but do think. If we are taken advantage of financially, it's usually because of lazy thinking—letting someone else think for you. Plan for yourself. Never make a major decision after the sun has gone down. Things look so much different in the daytime. Enjoy happy memories, but don't live in the past. Create a pleasant today.

If your children are grown, it's better not to live with them if it's at all possible. You need your independence and they need theirs.

If you find it necessary to live with your children, here are some suggestions. If you have sufficient money, you should contribute to your support—even if it's a small amount. If you have lots of money, be careful what you buy for them. Don't think you have to set them up so they can live like you think they ought. Let a married couple be one; don't treat one to something you know the other couldn't afford to do for them. In-law problems are sure to result if you do. Your attitude should be, "I want this home to be better because I am here." Set your limits for babysitting. You can't dedicate your life to their children. Learn balance.

To consider:
Which practical problems of life are most difficult for me now?
Do I expect others to solve them?
How can I bless those I need to receive from?

Another widow in Scripture is the woman in 2 Kings 4:1-8. Her story gives insight to us when we think we have nothing to go on with.

Many times when we pray we don't even know what we want. Crying is therapeutic, but it's not prayer. What do you want? What do you have in the house? We may say, "not much," but you have what you are, your smile, your attitude, etc.

We need to go borrow from somebody who has something. Are we willing to receive from others things we're lacking in ourselves? We get defensive easily with, "I'll never get hurt again. I'll be independent." But with that, we'll also be alone because it puts us in a cage or box which no one can penetrate.

God says get out of your cage and go to others, be vulnerable, and borrow lots—not a few, most of us live beneath our privileges. God has abundance for us and we want a little cupful. Don't be satisfied with just this. God wants so many more things for our lives. He wants us to experience fullness of joy, to walk in His wisdom, to stand before His presence, to be strengthened by His Spirit, living in light, unafraid of people and circumstances, at peace with ourselves and our family.

We have a responsibility to go out and let people increase us and benefit us and bless us—hollow us out, extend us, make us broader persons. We learn a little bit from one and a little bit from another and become enlarged persons, and then God can do more with us. We have a responsibility to go back into our homes with everything that we are. In God's family we can't afford to be too proud to admit our need or to receive from others.

We can't make anyone else responsible for what's going to happen in our homes and in our lives. It's between us and God. He has capacitated us for this. Shut the door. Begin to pour out what God has given you.

Pour forth to your children. Pour blessing and anointing in your home. As you pour, areas of your life become filled (vessels) and you don't feel emptiness and hollowness any more.

When one area of your life is filled, set it aside. It's taken care of. Don't worry about it or fuss over it any more. Pour out yourself—Christ in your life, the Holy Spirit in your life. As we receive from the Lord, we'll pour out as to the Lord; the more we pour out, the more we have left. Call for more, because now you're enjoying it.

In 2 Kings 4:6, we see the oil stayed. John 15:16 says your fruit shall remain. What we have is ours. We become spiritually wealthy and can pay our debts to society, to the past, present and future, and to the Lord. We shall live!

To consider:
When I've come to the end of my resources, can I stir myself from self-pity and reach out for love and strength?
Is it hard for me to believe I'll have a fruitful, enjoyable life? How can I find out?

Ministers' wives—women in ministry—women in leadership positions.

SECTION 9:

Service in the Church

The Minister's Wife

As a minister's wife, there are things you must consider in relation to your husband, and things to think about in relation to yourself.

It may seem your husband preaches beyond his living, but remember, it's God's Word, not his. Why is he tender and understanding with everyone else? Because they listen to him. First Samuel 1 reveals that Elkanah didn't understand Hannah, neither did Eli. Your complaint is, "All the women love him—and he loves it." Share wisdom and not jealousy. When it seems he is more interested in the "work" than home or you, join his interest, share his burden. God will put him in order.

Are you fighting or are you "perfect, thoroughly furnished" (2 Tim. 3:17)? Wives are to give to their husbands honor—both great and small (Esther 1:20). Check your attitude: Do you submit to your own husband

(Eph. 5:22)? Are you grave, not a slanderer, sober, faithful in all things (1 Tim. 3:11)? The way you live does make a difference (1 Pet. 3:1). There is a crown for the virtuous, the woman with strength of mind and/or body. No one has the effect on your husband that you have.

Absolutely refuse bitterness. Recognize him as your shepherd and headship and grow spiritually with him (2 Tim. 2:15). Communicate (not complain). You must learn how—be patient, it's worth it (Eph. 4:12-16).

Recognize your own assets. You have been called to God, to home, to ministry to others. (See Deut. 6:5-7; 1 Tim. 3:4-5; Titus 1:6-9.)

You have positional advantage as the "first lady" of the church. Look at your personal abilities, talents, rapport, hostessing, creative capacities, how you work with people, organize, teach, work with children, etc. (Matt. 22:37-38). Recognize your responsibilities. Know the difference between God's appointment and man's (Ezek. 44:10-16, 23). You are the ladies' example in all things—prayer, interest in sermons, motherhood, etc.

> Be thou an example of the believers, in word, in conversation, in charity, in spirit, in faith, in purity. (1 Tim. 4:12)

Remember, some talents can be developed.

Recognize your limitations. Acceptance is more than tolerance (Matt. 22:39). Get acquainted with yourself. You might be surprised. The source of your success is in

God. He will give you a new heart (Ezek. 11:19-20) and will give you one heart (Jer. 32:39-41). Where the Spirit of the Lord is there is liberty, not only for you, but for him (2 Cor. 3:17-18). Beholding Him we are changed.

> Not that I speak in respect of want: for I have learned, in whatsoever state I am, therewith to be content. I know both how to be abased, and I know how to abound: every where and in all things I am instructed both to be full and to be hungry, both to abound and to suffer need. I can do all things through Christ which strengtheneth me. (Phil. 4:11-13)

To consider:
Do I really believe God would not have put me in this position unless He gave me the capacity to do a good job? Am I willing to allow my husband to be less than perfect? To allow myself?

The Woman in Ministry
Ministry is servanthood. On the one hand, women are rolling up their sleeves to fight because they shouldn't have to serve in the home, and on the other hand, they are fighting for the right to be servants—longing to be accepted as clergy, to become ordained ministers and priests.

If you can do anything in life besides be in full-time ministry, do it. The blessings and rewards are unsurpassed, but the responsibilities of full-time ministry (pastoring, traveling teacher, etc.) should never be chosen by you as a vocation. Ministry is not a job; it's a way of life.

Don't choose the ministry for its glamor. It will destroy you unless you are divinely chosen and anointed for that service. It will crush the very thing in you that is motivating you to choose it, if that motivation is anything but the burning call of God.

The pressure of trying to accomplish God's work out of man's own strength is what is causing so many nervous breakdowns, heart attacks and ulcers in the ministry today. We are not equipped apart from God to meet spiritual needs. Trying to meet them via natural means destroys our ultimate faith in God. For as we fail, we begin to doubt Him, His ability, His promises. The very desire to help people is often turned into bitterness and cynicism.

As I understand it, you have a scriptural right to be a woman pastor. Women today want to move into this field because it has generally been a man's field and they are becoming aware that that was a limited understanding. Sometimes there is an underlying motive to prove that it was wrong, or to prove that women can function just the same as men, but if you can get out of it, don't do it. The cost is heavy.

If you are a minister, your greatest asset is your greatest liability. As women we are mothers, our maternal instincts permit us to know some things that no one else on earth can know—how to meet needs in a different way than men do, how to nurture and nurse people along, and how to feel problems before minds know what they are.

These assets can be liabilities because while we're bringing everyone to us and nursing them, all too often we refuse to do the weaning. As congregations grow, so do responsibilities. We can only give so much of ourselves. People are avidly attached to women pastors, as they meet so many needs in them. When we can rise in maturity levels and get beyond meeting our own needs in the ministry, we will delegate authority to others in whom God's Spirit dwells and relieve ourselves of duties God never intended for us to do. Men usually expect more of people than women do. This is an asset in helping people do for themselves.

God is restoring His church. He has given a hungering, thirsting spirit to many. People won't respond to lectures; we need to minister in the Spirit. By getting a theological degree, don't think you have the right to minister. Proverbs 18:16 points out that a man's gift makes room for him. Let the Word of Christ dwell in you richly (Col. 3:16). God's anointing will make a place for you. If God has placed His hand on you for full-time ministry, you won't be able to do anything but that. Once the deposit is of God, the doors are of God. It doesn't matter whether you have papers; you can't shut up the river of Life.

You are not ready to minister if you are trying to lay claim to a group for yourself—"my people, my church."

You're responsible to the Master and you must give an account to Him (Heb. 13:17).

If you aren't connected with a denomination, get the pastors in the area together and let them know what you are doing. Be teachable but not discouraged. Practice genuine humility. Recognize, as a woman, you have some vulnerable areas. You need the men in that city to know you are open to correction. That attitude will prompt acceptance and cooperation.

We are not called to bring new truth to the church, but to take truth already revealed and, with insight and ability as women, impart it to the body in a way it can be understood and appropriated.

Lay ministries work in the same way. Find your authority. Work within the realms of local authority; don't try to make a group or meeting be, simply let it be. You can't create a life-flowing group if life isn't flowing through you. If life is there, people will respond. If it's not, they won't, regardless of advertising or rituals. If God hasn't called you to pastor, no matter how many pastoral motions you go through you won't truly pastor a group.

Psalm 131:1 says, "Lord, my heart is not haughty, nor mine eyes lofty: neither do I exercise myself in great matters, or in things too high for me." This should be the prayer of every woman of God every day. "Don't let me try to walk like some superior I know, don't let me pretend that I know what I don't know. Let me be everything you've made me be, and let your deposit that's real come forth through me."

It's all for the glory of God whether it's milk or meat.

Don't let an ambitious spirit be your motivation for ministry. Guilt is a driving force that may contribute to a sense of ambition or a need to compensate by being and doing and going all the time. Jesus came to set us free from every curse and from every bondage.

If women have a deposit of God in them, then God will make a place for their ministry. If you are shut up in a place, then it's because God wants to raise that ministry level within you. He's producing something within you at this present time that will prevent the death of that if He lets you loose and you go out and share the same thing over and over again. If your ministry doesn't grow, it is evidence of a stagnated life. Your maturity should be evidenced long before it comes out of your mouth.

Our first and most important ministry is to our beloved Lord. As Mary poured the oil from the broken alabaster box and bathed Jesus' feet, so must we, from our own broken vessels, pour forth to Him our love and praise. This fragrance will permeate us and all about us.

Two verses often used against women ministering are 1 Timothy 2:11-12 and 1 Corinthians 14:34-35. Neither word translated silent means precisely that in Greek. *Hesuchia* and *sigao* mean with a quiet, teachable spirit, with a controlled tongue. It is the same word used in 1 Timothy 2:2, revealing a quiet and peaceable life, undisturbed by strife and discord. The word usurp means not to be domineering. It speaks here of an overbearing, demeaning control of her spouse.

Sometimes, because we are stirred within by an

awareness of a prophecy or a message in tongues given to us, we think we have to barge in with it the moment we become aware of it. To do so may be taking the control of a meeting out of the hands of the leader or interrupting one who is speaking. The Scripture says, "The spirits of the prophets are subject to the prophets" (1 Cor. 14:32), which means we are in control. We aren't forced to give it and, therefore, we don't become overbearing with a false sense of spirituality, insisting that we must give the word. We can pray and wait to see if the Lord will give opportunity for utterance.

Paul received ministry from women. We see Phebe (Rom. 16:1-2) who must have had a traveling ministry and Priscilla (Rom. 16:3) who with her husband tutored Apollos (Acts 18:2, 26) and had a church in her home (1 Cor. 16:19). In Philippi, Euodias and Syntyche were leaders of the church (Phil. 4:2). There were also deaconesses—which means a servant, helper, minister and those who minister the Word of the Lord. Corinthian women prayed and prophesied in the church. Romans 16:7 speaks of Junia, which could have been a woman apostle. In Acts 16:13 we see Paul attended women's prayer meetings. Paul obviously was not prejudiced against women in ministry.

Other Scriptures which reveal this same truth are Galatians 3:28, speaking of being neither male nor female but equal in rights and privileges regarding gospel benefits. Women were declarers of good news in Matthew 28:1-10; Luke 24:9-11; John 4:28-30 and John

20:16-18.

In Acts 2:14-21 and Joel 2:28-31, God promised women would be filled with His Spirit and would prophesy—speak to all people for edification, exhortation and comfort. (See 1 Cor. 4:1-6, 12, 24, 26, 29, 33.)

Philip's four daughters were prophetesses (Acts 21:8-9). Also Miriam in Exodus 15:20, Deborah in Judges 4:4, Anna in Luke 2:36, Huldah in 2 Kings 22:14 and other women gave prophecy (2 Chron. 34:22; Neh. 6:14).

In the New Testament many women ministered to Jesus. He raised the status of women and regarded the integrity of the person of women. Others thought them unable to learn, but Jesus taught them. He regarded them intellectually and spiritually.

We must realize that leadership carries with its privileges great responsibility, and merits our full consideration. May we as godly women be willing and delighted to be used of God, but never caught up in an ambitious spirit of self-promotion.

To consider:
How do I fit into God's plan for proclaiming His life?
Do I teach with a teachable spirit in my own self?
Do I remember that if a baby is not weaned, eventually the mother has nothing more to give—so I need to give healthy nurturing?
How have I failed to let go?

Women in Leadership

Submission to one another is taught in several Scriptures—1 Peter 5:5-11, Hebrews 13:17, 1 Corinthians 16:16 and Ephesians 5:21. Submission has nothing to do with the performance of the other person. (Committees should meet on an equal basis and go out from the meeting respecting each other's position.)

Leaders must intercede in word and deed. Romans 15:1 declares that the strong must bear the infirmities of the weak. Paul interceded for Onesimus to Philemon for love's sake. Peacemakers are blessed of God and shall be sons (Matt. 5:9) and we must carefully consider Matthew 5:47.

> And if ye salute your brethren only, what do ye more than others?

The confession of faults (James 5:16) must either be followed by prayer or criticism. We will do one of these—the choice is ours. As leaders, will we pray? Let the confessor's goal be healing. Our view of loving an enemy must be based on their condition—what's best for them.

Leaders must be involved in a ministry of reconciliation between man and God, man with himself, and man with man. In Nehemiah 1:4, though he was not personally involved with the remnant, he put himself with them in prayer—he wept, mourned, fasted and prayed. He followed prayer with action (Neh. 2:5).

Good leadership will give others opportunities, just as

the sun must throw off as much energy as is within or explode or invert and thus destroy. Inversion is all receiving and no giving. The Dead Sea has no outlet and thus is dead. Others must be allowed to give. God's people are many varieties and need a variety of ministries for balance. We must choose whether we want power or pedigree. Servants do not parade pedigrees—they offer service. As we feast on what He supplies, there's more than enough for all.

Starting in Matthew, chapter 2, we can follow Christ's example of preparation for leadership. In verse 1 we read of His miraculous or supernatural birth. This must be the starting place for each one of us. Following on, we see His obedience to authority, His baptism (Matt. 3:13) and His overcoming in temptation (4:1-11). Obedience to God's direction follows (4:12-16) and from then on Jesus began to preach.

The Bible specifically sets out for us qualities of leadership which are just as valid today as they were in the early days of Christianity.

Paul describes Timothy in Philippians 2:19-23, showing that a leader must reach out and take responsibility. In Judges 9:7-15, we see the fruit-bearing trees, which aren't interested in ruling over others, and the bramble, which isn't qualified but desires to rule. We should avoid leaders who reach for authority instead of responsibility, and who would be rulers over others (3 John 9; 1 Pet. 5:2-3).

A leader must have the ability to feed the flock (Jer.

3:15, 23:4; Ezek. 34:23; John 21:17; Acts 20:28; 1 Pet. 5:2) and gather the flock together (Isa. 40:10-11). This is contrasted with those who would fleece the flock (Zech. 13:7) and scatter them (Jer. 23:1-2).

A leader recognizes God's claim to both the sheep and the shepherd (Ps. 100:3; Ezek. 34:23; John 10:16) and doesn't try to claim the sheep for himself (1 Pet. 5:4; 1 Cor. 1:11, 3:3).

As leaders we can work out of the office or title of leader—or we can work out of our relationship with the Lord (Judg. 8:22-23).

Jesus specifically spoke against exercising dominion and authority over others. Matthew 20:25-27 emphasizes the attitude and function of servant to the extent of giving one's life for another. He beautifully illustrates this in John 13:4-17 in washing His disciples' feet.

There are two types of leadership: authoritarian, which uses "authority" to compel grudging obedience (Matt. 20:25), and inspirational, which inspires, persuades and sets example (Matt. 20:26-27).

The motive in leadership should be the desire to serve so that what I say and do and request is what is best for them. This also involves humility (Matt. 20:26-27)—to be chief you must be servant and willing to be the example (1 Cor. 11:1). There must be personal involvement.

What are qualifications for a leader? One must have vision (to be able to think ahead, plan and visualize) and imagination (for persons and plans). There must be the ability to set goals, both short- and long-range, which are realistic. A leader must have convictions and moral drive, and be able to make decisions (alert, to act quickly and aptly such as Jesus did when he saw the Temple being desecrated). Of great importance is the ability to delegate responsibility, knowing how to trust others while training them, prodding and organizing them with love and understanding, letting them be comfortable sharing ideas (i.e., never "put them down"). Finally, a leader needs self-discipline in working, planning, staff involvement and control.

One may function as a leader in the home—the miniature kingdom (1 Tim. 3:5)—in church, class, prayer group, work (superiors should be careful not to command what may reasonably be disobeyed), and in tomorrow's world. Jesus gave the final example of leadership:

> A new commandment I give unto you, That ye
> love one another; as I have loved you, that ye
> also love one another. By this shall all men
> know that ye are my disciples, if ye have love
> one to another. (John 13:34-35)

Leaders must first be sure a proper foundation is laid and take heed how it is built. First Corinthians 3:10 and Ephesians 2:18-22 speak of this. Paul points out that he preached Jesus Christ—Lord! Paul says to build not only for present gain but according to the grace which God gives. The word grace in Greek is *charis* and means commission, which includes the thought of God's enabling power.

Take heed how you build—you don't put a door on top of a roof. Be careful not to use short cuts (even though they may escape examiners), or improperly use people. Build with right doctrines. Three very valuable materials are to be part of the building: gold, which is true to the very center; silver, which is sound, good but not brilliant; and precious stones, used for ornamentation or stability (such as marble). These materials will abide judgment in this present life (Ps. 1:4-6) and the judgments of God (Rev. 20:11-15).

There are leaders and ministers whose own lives stand unimpeachable before God and man but whose service is worth little. Some have used the worthless materials, building poor and unstable structures of wood, hay and stubble. These cost little or nothing and will not endure—they are built out of pride, strife, envyings, false doctrines, divisions, bigotry, personal ambition, pride of talents, love of authority, love of praise and pride of denominations.

To consider:
Am I ruling or leading?
Am I delegating responsibility to others?
What quality in me needs developing if I am to show a house that will stand?

Giving practical counseling–receiving counsel–loneliness–discouragement–depression–forgiveness–deliverance–living with an alcoholic–those who are separated–marrying a divorced man–married to an unbeliever

SECTION 10:

When Help Is Needed

Giving practical counsel

There are guidelines we can follow to assist those in the Body of Christ who need help. We are dealing here with general counseling and not with those who need professional help, but the main thing to remember is that Jesus is the source of counsel.

> And the spirit of the Lord shall rest upon him, the spirit of wisdom and understanding, the spirit of counsel and might, the spirit of knowledge and of the fear of the Lord; And shall make him of quick understanding in the fear of the Lord: and he shall not judge after the sight of his eyes, neither reprove after the hearing of his ears. (Isa. 11:2-3)

We become partakers of that Spirit. His Word is our authority, His ways our experience. We have the example of Moses in Exodus 18:15-22, in particular, verse 19, where he is to *be* for the people. Romans 2:21-23 also brings this out.

We must check our motives regularly. It is important to stay within our own frame of reference and not just give idealistic answers, to pray for wisdom (James 1:5), not taking a clinical approach but with godly love, endued with the Spirit of God.

In setting the time for counsel, don't let the counselee set a time which is inconvenient for you. It is not necessarily spiritual to be inconvenienced. You have family and responsibilities which must be considered.

It has been said that a genuine crisis will last twenty-four hours; don't be manipulated by a cry for immediate help—"now or never." Trust the Holy Spirit's guidance in you as to whether you should drop everything in order to counsel. Often a few words can help to tide a person over until a satisfactory time can be arranged. Don't meet preceding a worship service unless absolutely necessary. Set a time limit and don't let it go on and on. Beware of chronics who seek "attention" but not help.

Genuine counseling is the giving of advice, not laying down laws. (See Prov. 11:14, 12:15, 13:10, 15:22.) As you listen, don't form an opinion too soon. Who's doing the talking determines what's said. Help them cut out details, but listen to what isn't being verbally said, too. You are not Solomon; be willing to say, "I don't know." Don't be forced into an immediate opinion—pray.

Ask questions which will help you get the needed information, not ones which will just satisfy your own curiosity. You don't need a blow-by-blow description of a tragic thing in their life. If you need more information, be sure your questioning is to give you a proper insight for study and prayer. If you begin to want the gory details, dismiss yourself as the counselor in that situation.

Draw from God's Word and your own experience. Don't be a Bible wired for sound—if they could have appropriated the Scripture verses, they wouldn't need you. Make the truths applicable to the situation.

Give them your faith. This is not wrong—but it *is* for a limited time. "I'll believe for you—for a week." This response causes their own faith to be stirred. Give them your prayers, both at the time of counsel and in the interim period. Give them your opinions, with reasons that make sense to their heads, not yours.

Let them reject your counsel or modify it any way they want to without reacting. It isn't necessary to force your opinions or guidance on them. It takes maturity not to, but if you aren't mature enough for that, you're not mature enough to counsel.

Encourage them in the future. Every time you see them, encourage them and show them love—but don't check on them regarding your counseling session. Let them be friends outside the counseling period. If you question them as to progress, you are likely to drive them away from you; you will be a constant reminder of their problem.

You may have to be a third party to reinstate broken communication, but beware of transferences or of becoming a lasting crutch. People are resilient—they need love and understanding, but not parenting. If God uses you for a period of time to counsel, say it, leave it alone, follow their lead and let the fruit be the Lord's.

To consider:
Have I prayed for love and wisdom to be available for counsel?
Can I treat confidences as precious, or is there something in me that wants to know others' problems for wrong reasons?
Do I force my opinions on others?

Receiving counsel
Not only do we need to know how to give counsel, but to receive it as well. There is scriptural validity in this, which encourages counseling as helpful guidance.

Psalm 1:1 says that the man who does not walk in the counsel of the ungodly is blessed. A limited understanding of this verse may cause us to think we should only receive advice from Christians. Yet, each of us is aware of the many teachers, employers and colleagues who shared their knowledge and experience with us in a counseling manner which benefited us greatly. Many of these people never professed to know

Christ as their Savior. Are we in error, then, to receive help from them? Certainly not. Psalm 1:1 is our guideline for measuring counsel, not counselors. All advice, help and counsel must be weighed in the light of God's Word. If it cannot agree, then it must be discarded as unacceptable, regardless of its logical content.

Here are eight practical suggestions for receiving counsel:

1) Pray first, before you ask counsel. Ask God to prepare you for the insights and answers you'll receive.

2) Make notes for yourself. Don't make the counselor play guessing games or have to weed out unnecessary conversation to discover the true need. Don't use this as an opportunity to impress your counselor with your knowledge—you are there for help.

3) Take notes. You will want to weigh the advice given with Scripture and it's difficult to remember when the session is over.

4) Ask questions. Don't presume you understand what has been said if you have any uncertainty. The counselor would rather know you understand what was actually said.

5) Be realistic about counsel. The counselor is not a miracle-worker, nor substitute parent, husband or wife. Counsel is not law, it's guidance.

6) Leave on time. If no specific time limit has been set before the session, leave when you have received the help you sought.

7) Be thankful. Express your gratitude to the person

offering you advice and then to God for His instrument in showing His wisdom and love to you.

8) Begin a course of action. Don't store the advice away somewhere and resume a "business as usual" attitude. Make some decisions. Ask the Lord to give you strength and courage to act—even if that action is to rest in His grace.

To consider:
Am I afraid to make choices?
Am I inclined to ask for help but continue in the same situation without acting?
Do I want someone else to make things right for me?

Loneliness
Loneliness can be time unfilled. What do we do with our time?

There are times of trauma when we reach out to others to come to us and be with us, but we must be careful that we don't usurp their time. Be aware they they have other responsibilities besides helping us. Be aware that their daily schedule may not be as flexible as ours (set meal times, children coming home from school, etc.). We must not take them away from their families for days at a time or even all their spare time.

Learn to contribute to others. Seek ways to bless and help others—physically and spiritually. Perhaps you can do some things that will free their time for other things.

Nighttime may breed or intensify fears and other

negative emotions in those who live alone. Plan your life accordingly—eat later, be careful what you watch on TV, etc. Plan toward a personal reward later in the evening, such as a bubble bath. Find an evening activity you can participate in, a sewing or painting class, for example.

Dag Hammarskjold was quoted as saying, "Pray that your loneliness will spur you on to find something to live for . . . something worth dying for."

To consider:
Is loneliness often a problem for me?
How do choices I make contribute to the problem of loneliness?

Discouragement
The English word for discouragement means to take away the courage of. The Hebrew word means to break down, cause to dismay (as in Deut. 1:21); to cut down, grieve, vex, trouble (Num. 21:4); make of no effect, neutralize (Num. 32:9); faint with fatigue, fear or grief, melt away (Deut. 1:28); and to crack in pieces, bruise, crush, struggle (Isa. 42:4). The Greek word means to be spiritless, disheartened (as used in Col. 3:21).

To prevent discouragement, you must nurture your faith when things are going well for you (Job 4:3-5). Predict and plan. Life isn't all surprises. Leave the world of chance and make plans. Stimulate interest for yourself in Christ and in others, learning and doing.

In dealing with discouragement, you must first admit it

to yourself. That is, affirm reality. Then honestly desire to be rid of it. You must assume the responsibility for your condition and the obligation to change it. Further, you need to encourage yourself. This word in Hebrew is *chazag* and means to fasten upon, seize, be strong, strengthen, cure, help, repair and fortify. It is used in Judges 20:22; 1 Samuel 30:6; 2 Chronicles 31:4, 35:2; and Isaiah 41:7. We're either stronger or weaker, healthier or sicker, as we come through grief, trials, problems and perplexities.

Courage must be regained. This is a command in many Scriptures: for example, Deuteronomy 31:6; Joshua 1:6, 10:25, 23:3; 2 Samuel 10:12; 1 Chronicles 19:13, 22:13, 28:20.

David dispelled discouragement in 1 Samuel 30:6 by encouraging himself in the Lord, his God. His situation was very discouraging. He had been rejected by the lords of the Philistines in chapter 29 and he then returned to find his city besieged by the Amalekites with the wives, sons and daughters taken captive and all his men turned against him. His method of encouragement is found in Psalm 69. In the first thirteen verses, discover the Lord. Let Him lift you (v. 29). Sing praise to Him (v. 30), magnify Him with thanksgiving and then declare victory (vv. 31-36).

That's all very well, but what about the discouragement that comes when you are guilty of wrong? Second Samuel 12 illustrates this for us. In verses 7-9, Nathan reveals David's sin agains Uriah; in verses 10-14, he declares

God's punishment and Bathsheba's child becomes very ill (v. 15).

There are nine steps revealed here (vv. 19-24):

1) Recognize death. Whatever you were involved with—it's over. Face it, it's finished.
2) Arise from the earth (repent). (See Psalm 51.) Turn away from it and move in the other direction.
3) Wash (take care of your appearance).
4) Anoint (receive a new touch of the Holy Spirit).
5) Change apparel (what you wear). How you appear to others *is* important. Let them see you not dragging around.
6) Go to the house of the Lord (for the atmosphere and fellowship).
7) Worship.
8) Eat at home (fellowship).
9) Encourage others.

To consider:

How can I avoid falling into discouragement?

How can what I've learned following discouragement help others?

Depression

To depress means to cast a gloom over, to dis-spirit. The word depression means to be in low spirits, gloominess, dejection. It is reported that four to eight million Americans are afflicted by serious forms of depression; one in two hundred will commit suicide. We must set ourselves free from hindrances, perplexities and embarrassments.

The common causes of depression are: pressure, guilt, fears (of not being useful, of people, of old age, of death), hate and unforgiveness (rejections and unresolved hurts), physical illness and fatigue, defeat (our attitude concerning failures and disappointments), stress (overload, finances, children, home problems), being taken advantage of, being wrongly related to God, self and others (spirit, soul and body), and Satan.

Second Corinthians 4:8-9 speaks to this problem. Let's look at this Scripture closely.

"We are troubled" means pressed or squeezed, which is the key to forming clay. It may be from rejection, illness, work or school pressures, oppressive authority, and life's limitations.

"We are perplexed" means to be, for example, like a ship without passage. This comes through death, loss, separation, failure in marriage or another area, etc. We don't know where to go—which way to turn.

We are cast down (i.e., as Satan was cast out of heaven). Every high thing that exalts itself against God must be cast down (demotions, leanness of soul). It's possible to be lowered without being humiliated (Judg. 15:9-20); this is despair.

But we are not distressed, that is, put in a straight, immovable place. This would be the absence of purpose.

We are not in despair (having no outlet whatever) and we are not forsaken (left down in). Jesus cried this to the

Father in Matthew 27:46, but it is not for us (2 Tim. 4:10, Heb. 13:15). He lifts us.

We are not destroyed, which is to be loosened away and perish. As the Phillips translation aptly says, we are knocked down but not out.

There are seven things involved in practical and spiritual release from depression:
1) Recognize the true situation, not merely the emotions of it, nor the accusations of it.
2) Wait on the Lord. If healing is delayed, let it be an occasion for growth and trust.
3) Change what you can, such as attitudes. If you will do this, God will prosper you. (See Ps. 1:1-3.) Depressed persons are often those who have learned how to be helpless.
4) Accept what must be. Refuse to pity yourself. As an individual you are unique and distinctive.
5) Forgive as Jesus did on the cross (Matt. 6:14-15).
6) Get joy (Rom. 15:13). It's impossible to have joy and remain depressed.
7) Give yourself totally to God and in love to others. Faith works by love (Gal. 5:6) and love dispels fear (1 John 4:18).

All depression is not satanic. We are equipped to handle a certain amount of stress, but we are not able to handle beyond a certain point without reaction. Stress can come from positives as well as negatives, from changes for good as well as upsetting changes.

The high degree of stress in normal living

circumstances today is the cause of a great deal of psychosomatic illness. The Christian's response is most likely to suppress it, because to react is not Christ-like. Pressure builds like a pressure cooker; if we don't blow the lid, we go into one mighty siege of depression.

What should we do? Make the divine exchange of Isaiah 61:3.

> To appoint unto them that mourn in Zion, to give unto them beauty for ashes, the oil of joy for mourning, the garment of praise for the spirit of heaviness; that they might be called trees of righteousness, the planting of the Lord, that he might be glorified.

We must first give it to Him, trade it to the Father. "I'm tired of praying over the past—sick of holding pity parties—sick of letting myself be put down by people—I give it to you."

To consider:
The Bible exhorts us to get joy—what are some ways I can do that?
How can I apply 2 Corinthians 1:3-4 to my problem of depression?

Forgiveness
Luke 6:27-38 shows we must be willing to forgive. Other Scriptures revealing this are Matthew 6:14, Mark

11:25, Luke 17:4, Ephesians 4:32 and Colossians 3:13.

We must be willing to forgive in order to be forgiven.

Acts 7:55-60 shows us how to forgive. We must be full of the Holy Spirit, looking steadfastly up (keep heaven's view before you), see God's glory, see Jesus as He is (glorified with the Father), declare your faith, commend your spirit to God, forgive and bless.

Joseph, in forgiving, won his brother, his father, and fame and fortune. Stephen forgave Saul and received an eternal reward.

We need more than just a feeling which will produce only a momentary forgiveness; we need more than just doing an act of forgiveness. We must lead a life of forgiveness.

When we truly acknowledge Jesus Christ as Lord and God as Father, we, the body, can truly say to God, "If he pleases you, he pleases me!"

Whoever is forgiven much, loves much (Luke 7:47).

To consider:

Why is it hard for me to forgive some people?

What price have I paid for withholding my love from those who have hurt me?

Deliverance

To be delivered from Satan, we must realize who he is. John 8:44 says he is the father of lies. His goal is to be independent of God and set himself up as an object of worship (Isa. 14:13-14). He counterfeits all reality. His devices include: sorcery, which is the practice of magic for Satan's benefit; fortune telling and lesser forms such as Ouija boards, crystal balls, fortune cards, horoscopes. (See Deut. 18:9-12.) Nearly all of Israel and Judah's problems can be traced to their involvement in the occult.

Once you realize who Satan is, come to Jesus. Denounce all involvement in the occult, including association with people in it, and get rid of its literature, objects, etc. Destroy them (Acts 19:18-19). Stay in the Word and fellowship with the saints. Actively, consistently, resist the devil (James 4:7-8). Satan may fight and tempt, but he must flee when you turn to Jesus and resist the devil.

We should curb our curiosity with the future and stay away from anything that endangers our faith. We are children of light and are not to learn the ways of darkness (Deut. 18:9; Ps. 81:8-9).

To be delivered from sin we must confess it and forsake it (Prov. 28:13; Rom. 8).

Deliverance from false teachers and prophets is ours as we check their doctrines with the Word and the Spirit. (See 2 Cor. 11:4, 13-15; 2 Peter 2:1-3; 2 John 10-11.)

If we will take the Lord's way, we can be delivered from temptation (1 Cor. 10:13; 2 Peter 2:9).

Trusting in the Lord releases from fear of death (2 Cor. 1:10; Heb. 2:15). Hold to the promises of God to keep from fear of old age (Isa. 46:4).

When we are in a strait place (imprisoned) and even in perplexities we bring on ourselves, deliverance is ours through prayer and praise (Acts 16:26; Jonah 1:17, 2:7-10).

To consider:
As a Christian, have I taken too lightly the command to keep away from the things of darkness?
Have I claimed in every area of my life the promise in John 16:33?

Living with an alcoholic

Alcoholics Anonymous is a tremendous program. It is not a church or religious organization, but it gets people ready for God to move in!

Generally the person who has a drinking problem, who drinks to excess, is a person with an exaggerated tender nature. This kind of person cares about a bug walking across the floor, a kitten who isn't being fed, the neighbor kids, everything in life. They have grown up caring and caring, and every time they looked around, they saw nobody seemed to share their feelings. Nobody but them seemed to care, and as they grew up in areas of life and became responsible as husbands, fathers, and on the job, they saw all these imperfections of life and became overwhelmed with them. They couldn't handle it so they used alcohol. In that state of intoxication they suddenly don't hurt any more.

It doesn't feel tender when he slams around, but then it's the defense against the tenderness. He's dealing with the man he wishes he was. He wishes he didn't care about anybody else, nobody else seems to. He wishes when he read the newspaper he didn't bleed inside over every negative. When he gets tanked up enough, he feels like that mean, cold-hearted person who represents society to him.

Why would God tell a wife or daughter to stay in this situation as a Christian? Because the only lasting hope for the alcoholic is the *agape* love of God, and He would leave her there to show it. His grace is sufficient.

The wife may cry, but she's not crying over today. She is always saying, "If he comes home drunk one more time, I don't think I can handle it." She can't—today. The program is: just stay sober one day at a time. The grace of God is given only for today. You have never had an unbearable day but you sure made some miserable ones worrying about it.

I don't believe God intends any woman to suffer physical abuse from her husband. Often the frustration locked inside an alcoholic becomes unleashed when he has been drinking, and is turned to violence. Leave if you see this building up in him. Do all you can to prevent his outbreak.

Never try to reason with him when he's intoxicated. If he'll permit you to put him to bed where he can "sleep it off," do it.

Remember that's not the true man who's flaring up at you, but rather the disturbed, frustrated one locked inside your loving husband. Jesus Christ is able to heal the inner man and calm the storm in his life. Believe God for this miracle in your home and in the meantime, love what you can.

To consider:
Can I put myself in the alcoholic's place and see the need for love?
Can I avoid self-pity and seek positive change in my own attitude?

Those who are separated

There are two questions for those who are unable to settle their marital status: For what purpose are you separated? Are you working toward reconciliation? Reconciliation means to change from enmity to friendship. Changes in *both* parties are necessary for friendship. Time alone won't change anything. There must be effort by both to discover the true problems and deal with them.

Marrying a divorced person

It takes a mature person to be able to accept that a divorced person has a responsibility towards those in the past, to allow him time and concern for "their" children. It takes maturity to see a check going out every month to those you're not involved with or caring about. It takes a mature person to know he has experienced marriage before and that he will have memories, to know that he may be making a comparison. This surely needs to be talked over.

You must be sure you can marry this person in faith for whatever is not of faith is sin.

To consider:
How would I counsel someone coming to me with marital difficulties? How does the world try to influence those who are separated or divorced? Can I search the Word and trust God's Spirit within me, or do I go from person to person seeking "law" to avoid responsible choice?

Married to an unbeliever
Second Corinthians 6:14-18 warns us of the inability of light to fellowship with darkness and forbids unequal yoking of believers with unbelievers.

Let us suppose that the wife received Jesus as Savior after her marriage and her husband has not, or that a Christian married an unbeliever in hopes he would soon become a Christian. Now that fellowship problems and a multitude of others have surfaced, should she divorce her husband?

The same Word which declares the above states in 1 Corinthians 7:10, "Let not the wife depart from her husband." Verse 13 states that the woman which hath an husband that believeth not, if he be pleased to dwell with her, let her not leave him. The remainder of verses 14-16 promise God's interest in the unbelieving husband because of the believing wife. It also strongly encourages the believer, that she may cause her husband's acceptance of salvation.

There has been much teaching to the Christian wife regarding her responsibilities to reveal Christ to her husband. Some have gone so far as to declare that if a husband isn't saved within a few months, the wife is failing. Let's keep the balance of thought. Every man must give account of himself to God. It is possible that when a woman lives lovingly and faithfully, displaying the graces of God in her life, her husband can enjoy these evidences yet refuse the Christ. The wife must not condemn herself for his decision.

Now let's view the other side of the issue. It *is* the responsibility of all believers to live before unbelievers in such a way as to stimulate interest in our Lord (1 Peter 3:15 and Phil. 4:5). Certainly the Christian wife has a desire for her husband to share her Lord, her friends and worship with her. Yet, this very desire can cause her to do and say things which literally turn him off. Can you imagine the embarrassment he feels when he opens his lunch pail and slips of paper on which Scripture is written cover his corned beef? Or having completed a heavy work schedule, he showers, slips into his robe and collapses into his favorite chair, reaching for the newspaper and finds instead a copy of *Logos Journal* all underlined in red pencil? The fact that she means well is little consolation to him at those times.

What if instead of Scriptures in his lunch he found "I love you" written on his napkin, or maybe just his favorite sandwich? When he sat in his chair, a cup of coffee handed him while he enjoyed reading the paper would speak of personal and loving concern.

Isn't it practical to believe that when Jesus Christ comes
into our lives we become better women, wives, lovers,
mothers, sisters? We change not by an ordered planning
on our part, but by allowing the Holy Spirit to perfect
that which concerns us (Ps. 138:8).

In counseling, I have seen a repeated mistake made by
Christian women married to unbelievers. In my own past
I was guilty of the same. That mistake is in making
husbands feel secondary to the main man in our
lives—Jesus. Listen to us as we describe or speak to Him.
"He's so precious, wonderful; He knows all about me; He
provides for my every need; He'll never let me down; I'm
His forever; He's my bridegroom." He is all this and
more but until your husband accepts and loves the Lord
Jesus as you now do, each statement is a threat to him as
surely as another man in your life would be. Even though
you may not say these things to your mate, it is likely that
he hears you as you share with your Christian friends in
person or on the phone; this further excludes him as one
who doesn't belong to your "club."

Every man wants to be precious to his wife, needs to
feel he knows her better than anyone else, that she
depends on him for provision and support and
faithfulness. How then should he feel about this Jesus
whom he views as an intruder?

James 1:5 promises wisdom to all who ask for it.
Certainly a wife needs daily wisdom to prevent negative
feelings in her husband about the Lord.

Practically, the wife can find spiritual fellowship at church, Christian women's meetings, etc. Sharing Jesus with friends can be done at times when your husband is involved with things or persons other than you.

If her fellowship needs are being met with Christians and the personal times with her Lord have allowed her to express her love to Him, the wife should be able to spend time with her husband doing and discussing things which are of interest or importance to him without feeling less "spiritual."

Laughter, fun and pleasure are ingredients that spice our lives and prevent dullness. Let us be cautious that we don't lay these aside in the name of Christianity. Jesus said, "I am come that ye might have life and have it more abundantly."

One of the beautiful lessons we learn from the life of our Lord is that He began with people where they were. Or as we say today, He knew where they were coming from. To Peter, He spoke of fish, to Nicodemus, He spoke of law.

What is important to your husband, if it does not violate God's Word or your personal integrity, is what must become important enough to you to become involved, at least in interest.

Jesus did not enter your life to replace your husband. He came to bless and unite the marriage in every way by showing you a love far beyond any you've ever experienced. In your receiving from Him, you have the privilege of sharing that love with your companion in tangible ways he can and will receive.

To the unbeliever who isn't involved in church, weekends are viewed as a time of pleasure. Monday through Friday conversations focus on the weekend plans. To the man whose wife begins planning for Sunday all day Saturday by studying her Bible lessons, ironing Sunday clothes, etc., little excitement remains. He is left with the choice of doing things alone, finding someone other than his family to share his time off with, or doing nothing but wait for Monday to roll around so he can return to work.

The wise wife plans early for her worship day so she may be available to her husband for companionship on the weekends.

It isn't an isolated case in which the wife has actually given up church attendance on a particular Sunday, gone fishing or camping for the weekend and found the next weekend her husband willing to accompany her to church.

Ways of showing love need not always demand such compromise. I have learned that many husbands like to have their wives with them when they wash the car, weed the yard, or paint a room. Just the fact that you take the time to be with him is an evidence of love.

What works for one couple may not for you but don't give up. "Faith without works is dead, being alone." Keep pouring and soon you'll find your husband's cup being filled, his needs being met by God's love through you. More amazing, you'll not have been drained or depleted in any way, for the more you give, the more He gives to you.

God's grace will enable you to be a living vessel pouring forth God's love; ask for His wisdom to be meted out to you daily, giving guidance and direction as to how and when to pour and the joy of Jesus will be the light in your home.

What is the Worth of a Woman?

It's the delight of knowing God created us
with the mentality to govern ourselves
in every role of womanhood—

the freedom of emotional response
to beauty, love, grief and pain—

the strength to pursue that which is valuable—
to endure that which is necessary
and to shun that which is not for us—

the joy of mothering
whether or not we give birth to children—

the peace of accepting ourselves
as first, not second class citizens
and the security of knowing we are children
of the most high God,
who loves and cares for us,
and with whom we shall live eternally.

For free information on how to receive
the international magazine

LOGOS JOURNAL

also Book Catalog

Write: Information - LOGOS JOURNAL CATALOG
Box 191
Plainfield. NJ 07061